An Introduction to the History of Education

Richard Aldrich

HODDER AND STOUGHTON

LONDON SYDNEY AUCKLAND TORONTO

British Library Cataloguing in Publication Data

Aldrich, Richard
  An introduction to the history of education.—
  (Studies in teaching and learning)
  1. Education—England—History
  I. Title   II. Series
  370'.942   LA631

ISBN 0 340 26293 1 Paperback

First published 1982

Typeset by Graphic Consultants International Ltd, Singapore.
Printed and bound in Great Britain for
Hodder and Stoughton Educational,
a division of Hodder and Stoughton Ltd,
Mill Road, Dunton Green, Sevenoaks, Kent,
by Richard Clay (The Chaucer Press) Ltd, Bungay, Suffolk.

Contents

Studies in Teaching and Learning

The purpose of this series of short books on education is to make available readable, up-to-date views on educational issues and controversies. Its aim will be to provide teachers and students (and perhaps parents and governors) with a series of books which will introduce those educational topics which any intelligent and professional educationist ought to be familiar with. One of the criticisms levelled against 'teacher-education' is that there is so little agreement about what ground should be covered in courses at various levels; one assumption behind this series of texts is that there is a common core of knowledge and skills that all teachers need to be aware of, and the series is designed to map out this territory.

Although the major intention of the series is to provide general coverage, each volume will consist of more than a review of the relevant literature; the individual authors will be encouraged to give their own personal interpretation of the field and the way it is developing.

Preface

This book provides six perspectives upon the history of education in England and Wales. The basic dimensions of society which underlie education — family, gender, occupation and others — are first identified. Ideas and ideals are considered next: Christian, societal, individual, literate and universal. The third chapter introduces the organisation and workings of the formal educational system. Controlling bodies, teachers and examinations are used to provide insights into the several parts of this process.

The second half of the book is concerned with primary, secondary and higher education. These terms, however, are not used in a contemporary sense. For example, primary education is not simply to be equated with twentieth-century primary schooling. Primary education is defined rather as fundamental or basic education: an education neither essentially institutional nor confined to a particular age range. Chapter Four is the history of different attempts to supply this need.

Unlike many other histories of education which cover only the last two hundred years the time span of this book is a lengthy one. The final chapters are each divided into three sections. These are the medieval origins, early modern period, and nineteenth and twentieth centuries. Such wide-ranging treatment is essential if contemporary society and education are to be seen in their true perspectives. Historical understanding involves some appreciation not only of the world we have made but also of those we have lost.

Acknowledgments

Denis Lawton guided this book in its early stages. The comments and criticisms of Margaret Bryant, Dennis Dean, Peter Gordon and Harold Silver have saved me from many errors of fact and judgement. My wife, Averil, has typed the manuscript. Bernadette Newman has seen the book into print.
To these, and many others, my thanks are due.

London, 1982   Richard Aldrich

1 Introduction

This chapter examines some of the basic social and economic dimensions of human existence within which a history of education must be located.

Family

The family is the most permanent and immediate educational unit. For centuries in this context children have learned the first essential social, economic and cultural skills. These have included speech — the most basic means of communication — and a wide variety of activities ranging from toilet training through household duties to bedtime prayers. Moral, social and vocational training formed the basis of this domestic curriculum, but rudimentary literacy skills were also learned in the family just as they are today. Historically speaking the family clearly predates schooling and will perhaps outlast it. It is the natural means of rearing the young as practised by higher mammals, and, in the extended human family relationships characteristic of societies less mobile than our own, parents, grandparents, elder brothers and sisters, aunts, uncles and other relations have been the chief teachers of the young. Thus each individual is as a child a learner, and, as an adult, potentially a teacher too. When families or friends failed, usually as a result of death or dire poverty, the parish or other body assumed responsibility, either through a substitute family or through workhouse or other charitable provision.

Limitations of family education were recognised and catered for in a variety of ways. Thus in the medieval period, for example, it was customary for some boys and girls to be brought up in families other than their own. The establishment of a great noble or of a wealthy gild master could supply a fuller educational experience than was obtainable in humbler homes. Here pages and squires on the one hand, and apprentices on the other, acquired social and cultural as well as vocational skills. The system operated at several levels of society. Thus the successful eighteenth-century handloom weaver might add a poor apprentice or two to be brought up as members of a humble but sober, God-fearing, autonomous family economic and educational unit.

Schooling was another means of replacing or of supplementing family education. In the case of workhouse or charity schooling it might be a complete institutional substitute, though leading ultimately to some form of apprenticeship or other relocation within a family. Recourse to schooling might be for short periods only to supply particular deficiencies. Literacy skills and accomplishments of various kinds might be acquired outside the family either when needed, or as time and finance permitted. Day schooling, even where hours and attendance were regular, still saw children basically located in the family. Where boarding took place pupils usually became part of the master's family and lodged in the master's house.

In the nineteenth century the concept of the educative family retreated in the face of the rise of the schooled society. For many ordinary folk the decline of domestic education coincided with the decline of the domestic economy. The one was replaced by the school, the other by the factory or office. Thus the monitorial system was likened by contemporaries to the steam engine. Lancaster and Bell provided a new efficiency in education based on a new division of labour. Self-instruction was to be the key whereby one master might even supervise a thousand pupils or more.[1]

The transition from family to school was a complex one and involved changes of emphasis spread over many decades. But family education was significantly affected when parents, and/or children, were daily employed for very long periods in factory and mill. In such situations infants and young children who might otherwise have been nurtured at home must be put out to schools or childminders to be dosed with a variety of palliatives ranging from education to Godfrey's cordial. By the mid-nineteenth century, however, as the report of the Newcastle Commission indicated, schooling of some sort was the norm for the mass of the population. Family rights in education continued, particularly whilst parental 'pence' contributed a significant proportion of school incomes. Ultimately, however, such issues as attendance, curriculum and standards became matters of governmental, bureaucratic and professional concern and control.

The decline or redrawing of the domestic education of the upper classes in the nineteenth century can be explained in several ways.

The tutor retreated, to be replaced by the nanny and the governess. Preparatory, proprietary and public schools flourished as never before. Prestigious headmasters, a new social ethos and exclusiveness, a new seriousness in work, play and moral discipline were all contributory factors. So too were the developing railway and postal services. But above all, it has been argued, domestic education is the education of a relatively static and traditional society. The aspiring *nouveaux riches* of the nineteenth century had their sons and some of their daughters educated not in their own homes nor in the homes of their social superiors, but in the schools of those social superiors, or in schools modelled closely upon them.

In the twentieth century the family has undergone further significant change. Its breakdown has been facilitated by the Divorce Reform Act of 1969, although marriage (including remarriage) remains as popular as ever. New family models have been provided by immigrant communities. Today very few families educate their children without recourse to schooling. Indeed legislation has made it almost impossible for them to do so. Nevertheless family influence upon education remains strong, and is a major factor in determining children's performance at school.[2]

Gender

Males and females have been accorded different roles and status in English society. Educational provision, and the writing of history of education has reflected these differences.

The medieval period was a time of role differentiation and male domination in many respects, not least in matters of religion and the church. Nevertheless the scattered nature of settlement and difficulties of communication probably produced significant local variations in custom and practice which have gone largely unrecorded.

Medieval discipline was strict, and corporal punishment common-place for girls as for boys. Medieval crafts were primarily carried on by males but girls were also apprenticed in embroidery and similar occupations. From the early modern period, however, 'parish apprentices' might include boys and girls in equal numbers. Throughout English history the domestic role, and consequently domestic education, has been considered more appropriate for girls than boys. Thus in the Middle Ages where girls attended petty or English schools they probably did so in fewer numbers and for shorter periods than their male counterparts.

Some girls of wealthier parentage, like boys, were educated in the homes of the nobility. Though formal training in martial arts was doubtless denied to them, domestic duties, social accomplishments, moral and religious training and some literacy skills formed a broad basis of educational experience. The church and the law were male professions, and the educational establishments connected with them — the universities, inns of court and grammar schools — were for males. In the medieval period though there were instances of girls attending grammar schools this was possibly to acquire reading and writing skills in English rather than in Latin.

Nunneries, like monasteries, were responsible for the training of their novices. Their schools also provided some day and boarding education for those not intending to enter the cloisters. Nunneries supplied girls and younger boys with religious and moral training, though scholastic opportunities were less than in the monastic schools.

Dimensions of female domesticity and male vocationalism have continued to influence educational provision from the medieval period until the twentieth century. Insofar, however, as workhouse and charity schools of the early modern period sought to inculcate habits of religious observance, morality, obedience and industry into poor and destitute children, such principles could be applied to both sexes. It was important that girls as well as boys should learn how to support themselves and to refrain from criminal acts, in order that they should not become a further burden on the parish. A general curriculum of endeavour, obedience and right conduct was applicable to all. Boys might also be trained in skills applicable to local employment. Girls would be taught domestic skills and duties, useful for the roles of both servant and housewife, as well as traditional female crafts connected with clothing manufacture.

Similarly, in the nineteenth- and twentieth-century elementary schools, a general concern for the moral and religious welfare and basic literacy of the working classes predominated. There were curricular differences, cookery and dressmaking for girls, wood-work for boys, but legislation for compulsory school attendance included boys and girls on equal terms.

Sixteenth-century England, the England of Queens Mary and Elizabeth, furnished several examples of highly educated, even scholarly, women. Modern and classical languages now became accepted subjects of study for some girls of the upper ranks of society. But in spite of sixteenth-century humanism, and advocates of education for all regardless of sex, role differences still determined the nature of educational provision. Basic literacy, household management and social accomplishments were the staple curriculum for well-bred girls whether educated in domestic establishments by family and tutors, or in private day or boarding schools and academies. Female monarchs, daughters, sisters, wives and mistresses notwithstanding, the areas of politics, church, law, medicine, army, navy, agriculture, industry and commerce were male preserves, as were the educational institutions from which their ranks were supplied. Not until the twentieth century did women in significant numbers even begin to gain equal access to these worlds.

Rank, order, class

'Rank', 'order' and 'class' are but three of the many terms which have been used to indicate the complex divisions of English society. Medieval society had three broad male dimensions, those who prayed, those who fought and those who toiled, dimensions still reflected centuries later in such feudal survivals as the Estates General which met in France until 1789. Today's official social classification still takes account of employment, wealth and status, three bases for division and identification in societies throughout history.

For centuries children have been educated principally in accordance with their positions in society. Thus sons and daughters of noblemen would receive an education different from that of the children of labourers or serfs. The tutorial systems of education advocated by Locke[3] in the seventeenth century and Rousseau[4] in the eighteenth were by definition for the few, not for the many.

Yet education has also been a significant means of social mobility. However stringently in the interests of social stability, sons are channelled into their fathers' occupations the system breaks down where confronted, as in the medieval period, by the existence of a celibate clergy. Thus in *Piers Plowman* Langland recorded how 'a beggar's brat can become a bishop, and sit among the peers of the realm and lords' sons and knights crouch to him'.[5]

Some successful schools and colleges of the medieval and early modern periods, however, were diverted from their original purposes by the intrusion of sons of the nobility and gentry. Thus in 1382 Winchester College was founded by William of Wykeham 'for ever to consist in and of the number of seventy poor and needy scholars'. Similarly New College, to which old Wykehamists would proceed, was to be 'a perpetual college of seventy poor scholars, clerks, to study theology, canon and civil law and arts in the University of Oxford'. By the sixteenth century foundations such as these were becoming the preserves of the wealthy, a process accelerated by the establishment of the Anglican Church which legitimized the practice of clerical dynasticism.

The social changes which accompanied the classic period of the industrial revolution have been well charted by such writers as H.J. Perkin, *The Origins of Modern English Society, 1780–1880* (1969), N.J. Smelser, *Social Change in the Industrial Revolution* (1959), and E.P. Thompson, *The Making of the English Working Class* (1963). There was a rash of new educational ventures — Sunday schools, monitorial schools, mechanics' institutes and the like — many of them designed to cater for the educational needs of the new urban proletariat.

In the early nineteenth century the development of industrial production and a class-based society resulted in the further decline of the world of yeoman and artisan. William Cobbett[6] was the pugnacious but unavailing champion of this world and of its educational traditions, formal and informal. Other radicals, including Owenites[7] and Chartists[8] also tried to shape an educational experience which would protect the labouring classes from the worst excesses of political, industrial and religious exploitation. This alternative system was intended to supply 'really useful knowledge'. Its agencies included a free press, itinerant lecturers and discussion centres. Informed parents would thus ensure that the home remained a true educational agency. Schools would not be subservient to the interests of a corrupt church and a tyrannical government. Indeed one of the overall purposes of such educational provision was to secure the reform of these two institutions. By the middle of the nineteenth century, however, the failure of these alternatives was apparent and the children of the working classes were shepherded into the official schooling system.

Education of the sons (and later the daughters) of the middle classes prompted reforms in grammar schools and universities, and found particular expression in the public school. Entry to the boys' public schools of the nineteenth and twentieth century was restricted by an admissions system based on wealth and patronage. In a classic threefold initiation process sons of the wealthy were firstly separated from their parents into boarding schools. There they were hardened physically and mentally by a ritualised system of beatings, fagging and the games cult on the one hand, and classics on the other. Finally, equipped with the identification symbols of public school accent, esoteric knowledge and old school tie, they proceeded into the adult world. The success of this exclusive, self-perpetuating system is shown by the high proportion of ex-public school boys amongst Cabinet ministers, bishops, judges, senior civil servants, generals and the like.

In the twentieth century education both inside and outside schools still reflects rather than determines social class. Attempts to reverse this relationship have concentrated upon the secondary stage — equal access to publicly provided schools, and the principle of a common school. Alternatives to schooling have had little success, whilst the social division between those who pay for the private schooling of their children at both primary and secondary stages and those who do not remains one of the most distinctive features of English education.

Population

Population figures prior to the nineteenth century must be treated with extreme caution.[9] The population of Anglo-Saxon England had probably doubled to about three million by the mid-fourteenth century when outbreaks of plague consequent upon the Black Death of 1348–9 reduced the total by about a third. By 1600 it had doubled again to some four million.

Estimates of the population of England and Wales in 1700 range from five to six million, and for 1750 from six to six and a half. Since 1801, apart from 1941, decennial censuses have been taken. The first showed a population of some nine million which had doubled to eighteen by 1851 and doubled again to 36 million by 1911. From 1801 to 1911 the decennial increase was never less than 10 per cent, a figure probably never exceeded at any other time in English history. In contrast it should be noted that the population of Ireland, which in 1841 exceeded eight million, steadily declined to under four and a half million by 1911.

The increase was most apparent in the booming commercial and industrial centres. Between 1801 and 1911 the population of Bradford rose from 13,000 to 288,000, of Cardiff from 2,000 to 182,000, of Sheffield from 46,000 to 455,000, of Southampton from 8,000 to 119,000.

The causes of this population explosion have been much discussed. Improved fertility, diet, clothing, sanitary and medical care, the value of children as sources of income and as insurance in old age have all been adduced. The results, however, are easier to assess. Increases such as these brought into question traditional means of educational supply, particularly inasmuch as they resulted in a high proportion of young people. In 1851 about one quarter of the population were under ten years old. A century later that fraction had declined to less than a sixth.

Many children and young persons found employment. In the late eighteenth and early nineteenth centuries pauper apprentices and other youngsters constituted a high proportion of the workforce in many of the new factories. By the 1860s, however, except in domestic service, employment opportunities for children, even in traditional areas like agriculture, were in relative decline.

In the twentieth century the population has continued to increase in spite of two world wars and some significant changes in the patterns of child bearing. Nevertheless two current reversals of nineteenth-century trends may be noted. The first is the ageing of the population. The bulge is no longer amongst those who have not yet begun to work, but rather amongst those whose working lives are completed, or suspended. Secondly the recent problem of declining school rolls is frequently most keenly felt in those very urban areas which witnessed the most rapid nineteenth-century growth. In the last decade Inner London, for example, has lost nearly twenty per cent of its inhabitants. In 1981 the population of England and Wales stood at 49 million, a mere half a per cent increase over the 1971 figure.

Investment and Consumption

Over the centuries education has been seen as an important means of investment. Parents at all levels in society have diverted often scarce economic resources into securing the best possible education for their children. Modern studies would appear to confirm that such investment bears fruit. Thus, for example, it has been shown that in the USA on average college graduates earn more than high school graduates. Similarly in poorer countries those with secondary schooling on average earn more than those with primary schooling, who in turn earn more than those with no formal schooling at all.

It is impossible, however, to generalise from such studies and to project these findings backwards through history. If those who proceeded to more education were the more able, determined, or better patronised, they might well have secured higher average earnings even had their education been restricted. Secondly, historically speaking, access to longer periods of formal education has depended upon a variety of factors, social, economic, vocational, regional. The extended schooling of the medieval cleric did not necessarily ensure for him a higher standard of living in this world than that of the landowner.

Thirdly, formal educational qualifications and experience now have a general currency in terms of selection for employment which is of relatively recent standing. Thus today a combination of school leaving certificates, a first degree or a higher degree may be used as basic qualifications for entry into a variety of well-paid occupations. In former times however, particularly prior to the development of an extensive examination structure, such appointments would have been made by patronage, influence, or simply by sale and purchase.

In the eighteenth century Adam Smith[10] outlined the national benefits to be secured by state intervention in education. This, he believed, would render the nation's citizens more orderly, rational and responsible. Nearly one hundred years later Britain's poor showing at the Paris exhibition of 1867 caused Lyon Playfair[11] to warn that the growing industrial challenge of such countries as Prussia, France and Belgium stemmed directly from their superior educational systems. Though Playfair's conclusions have been debated from that day to this, in 1963 the influential study of Bowman and Anderson showed a highly significant correlation between basic adult literacy rates and national wealth.[12]

Once again, however, such findings must be treated with extreme caution. Correlation does not necessarily mean causation. Literacy is as difficult to measure as it is to define, and comparisons across different cultures and periods of time are fraught with danger. National wealth can be transformed by factors which are unrelated to education; on the one hand by the discovery and exploitation of oil or precious metals, on the other by war or pestilence, or by a political regime with a 'back to the jungle' philosophy.

Education has also to be seen in terms of private and public consumption. For example some nineteenth-century artisans chose to spend their hard won money on library subscriptions, evening classes, or 'superior' schools for their children. Some of the wealthier middle classes sent their sons to expensive public schools and dispensed with the services of a few grooms, gardeners, housemaids or governesses. Similarly, in the twentieth century some nations have consciously devoted a higher proportion of their resources to education, and less to such items as defence or roads, or vice-versa.

Historians have frequently drawn attention to the growing public expenditure on education during the nineteenth and twentieth centuries. This usually takes the form of a steady progression from the £20,000 grant of 1833, though punctuated with a series of retrenchments as in the Revised Code of the 1860s.[13] In 1950–1 a sum equivalent to 3.1 per cent of the Gross National Product of the United Kingdom was spent on education. By 1972–3 this percentage had doubled, and in 1977–8 exceeded 7 per cent, an expenditure of more than £7,000 million.[14]

Occupation

For most of English history land was the prime source of wealth and occupation, with human habitation broadly scattered upon it. During the nineteenth century, however, the social and economic context of education was radically altered as many parts of England and Wales were rapidly urbanised and industrialised. In 1841 agriculture, horticulture and forestry claimed 1,434,000 of the 5,093,000 occupied males in Great Britain, the largest single category of employment. That total rose for a decade and then steadily declined to just over the million mark by the middle of the twentieth century when the total of occupied males exceeded fifteen and a half million. In 1901 there were more males employed both in metal manufactures and in transport and communications than in agriculture. By 1871 there were more females in domestic offices and personal services than males in agricultural employment.

In 1801 a third, in 1851 a half, and by 1901 three quarters of the population lived in towns. As a result English education also became urbanised. Educational provision in pre-industrial, pre-urbanised England, that 'world we have lost',[15] was shaped by forces and priorities less familiar to us today. It was local rather than national, diverse rather than uniform, here domestic, there institutionalised, here flourishing, there in decay. In rural areas it took firm account of season, harvest, distance, weather, and economic necessity. The children of itinerant workers, the tramping artisan, peddlars, showmen, gypsies and the like, those with no fixed abode, would naturally have no fixed place of education.

Thus until the nineteenth century, urban occupation, society and schooling were the exception rather than the norm. The capital differed again from other cities and towns both in degree and kind. Even in 1801 when the population of London exceeded a million, no other town in England and Wales was a tenth of that size, and only five, Birmingham, Bristol, Leeds, Liverpool and Manchester had more than 50,000 inhabitants.

Formal schooling in this country has strongly vocational origins. Monasteries and nunneries were responsible for securing a supply of novices and for their training. Medieval schools whether monastic, cathedral or collegiate church in origin were training grounds for clerics in such professional skills as song, Latin grammar, theology and canon law. Similarly the earliest European universities were concerned with professional knowledge, medicine at Salerno, law at Bologna. Oxford and Cambridge provided basic arts courses, and a master's degree became the professional qualification for teacher and cleric.

Clerical control in grammar schools and universities survived in this country until the nineteenth century. In 1825 the *Westminster Review* deplored the continuation of a system whereby, 'Tailors educate tailors, and boatswains seamen, but the clergy of Britain educates statesmen and lawyers and soldiers and merchants and physicians'.[16] University College, London, founded in 1826 without any apparatus for religious control, teaching or curriculum, provided a new context for the study of such fields as architecture, engineering and medicine.

Medieval education was basically vocational education, and schooling a means of preparing for one group of occupations. Elementary schooling for all in the nineteenth century, and secondary schooling for all in the twentieth, have been justified in part in terms of supplying basic survival and employment skills in the more complex social and economic systems of today. They have also, however, served to keep young people out of the labour market, and have themselves provided a means of employment for a considerable number of educated people.

Conclusion

Family, gender, class, population, investment and consumption and occupation have not merely influenced the history of education in

England and Wales. They have in large part constituted it. Society and education are inextricably interwoven.

Thus the highly specialised and professional society of the second half of the twentieth century has naturally been reflected in a highly specialised and professional educational system. This, however, has made it more difficult to appreciate the significance of the non-specialised and non-professional dimensions of society and education both in the past and in the present.

NOTES

1   **The monitorial system,** its founders Joseph Lancaster (1778–1838) and Andrew Bell (1753–1832) and the Newcastle Commission, are examined in Chapter 4.

2   *See* for example, J.W.B. Douglas, *The Home and the School* (1964) and G.W. Miller, *Educational Opportunity and the Home* (1971).

3   **John Locke** (1632–1704), philosopher, tutor, writer, university don, physician and public servant.

4   **Jean-Jacques Rousseau** (1712–78), French political writer and educationist, author of *Emile* (1762).

5   **Quoted** in D.W. Sylvester, *Educational Documents 800–1816* (1970), p. 48. Wherever possible references are given to easily accessible collections of documents.

6   **William Cobbett** (1763–1835), author of *Rural Rides* and publisher of the *Political Register.*

7   **Followers of Robert Owen** (1771–1858) pioneer socialist of Welsh origin whose ideas were implemented in various experiments in England, Scotland and the USA.

8   **Chartism,** which flourished in the years 1838–48, included amongst its objectives the principle of a vote for every man.

9   Statistics in this chapter are taken from B.R. Mitchell and P. Deane, *Abstract of British Historical Statistics* (1962).

10   **Adam Smith** (1723–90), Scottish economist, author of *The Wealth of Nations* (1776).

11   **Lyon Playfair** (1818–98), scientist and Liberal politician.

12   **M.J. Bowman and C.A. Anderson,** 'Concerning the role of education in development' in C. Geertz (ed.), *Old Societies and New States* (1963). This and other contemporary and historical comparisons of income and literacy rates are examined in M. Blaug, *An Introduction to the Economics of Education* (1970), Chapter 3, 'The Contribution of Education to Economic Growth'.

13   In 1860 the various regulations or minutes of the Committee of the

Privy Council on Education were consolidated into a code. The so called Revised Code of 1862 replaced the previous system of specific grants for separate purposes. Henceforth a single block grant would be payable to the school managers. One third would be dependent on the numbers of pupils in attendance, the further two thirds upon the performance of pupils in an annual examination in reading, writing and arithmetic (the 3Rs). See N. Morris, 'Public Expenditure on Education in the 1860s', *Oxford Review of Education* (1977), 3(1), for details of the scheme and its effects.

14 **K. Fenwick and P. McBride,** *The Government of Education* (1981), p. 63.

15 *See* P. Laslett, *The world we have lost* (1965).

16 *Westminster Review* (1825), 4, p. 169. The *Westminster* was the leading radical quarterly of this period.

2 Ideas and Ideals

Human history is essentially a history of ideas and ideals, with the history of education a key dimension in this story. Education both reflects and disseminates ideas and values current in society. It also helps to create and reformulate them. Thus throughout history children and others have been initiated into the developing, prevailing, or outmoded, intellectual, moral, religious and social ideas and ethos of their society or group. At the same time many of those connected with education, including the traditional 'great educators', Plato, Aristotle, Augustine, Aquinas, Comenius, Locke, Rousseau, Newman and Dewey,[1] have influenced not only the educational thought and practice of their times, but also the very history of thought itself. Thus in *An Essay Concerning Human Understanding* (1690), John Locke rejected the doctrine of innate ideas, held in various forms for some two thousand years. He argued instead that knowledge proceeded from experience, conveyed through the senses, and ordered by reflection and reason.

The concept of education has been changed throughout history. At present the popular notion includes, indeed to a considerable extent is dominated by, the largely state-provided apparatus of free, universal, compulsory schooling for all children aged 5 to 16, with further elaborate institutional provision for large sections of the age cohorts up to 18 and 21 years of age. This concept is of recent historical vintage, indeed the ideal of secondary education for all is still being defined and implemented, particularly in the context of the comprehensive school. Education, however, may be viewed from many standpoints: as a service provided by the state, as the right of the individual, as a means to a variety of ends, as an end in itself. Or again, education has been defined as initiation into worthwhile activities. The purpose of this section is to identify some of the historical answers to the question, what is education, and what is educationally worthwhile.[2]

Christian Ideals

Most societies have had some idea of a god or gods, and of a world, if not a life, after death. This phenomenon may be explained in several ways. Some would interpret it as a series of different historical manifestations of an essential supreme being. Others would point rather to a perpetual need to account for the inexplicable and unknown, or the desire to give a richer meaning to existence than the mere threescore years and ten spent upon this earth. The Christian concept of that supreme being, God the Father, God the Son and God the Holy Ghost, and of an after life in Heaven or Hell, has predominated in England and Wales throughout most of their recorded history.

The major divisions which emerged in the Christian church in the west in the sixteenth century, have lasted until this day. Judaism apart, however, other religions than Christianity have had little place in English society, until the advent of large scale Commonwealth immigration, particularly from the Indian sub-continent in the second half of the twentieth century. Thus educational ideas have been construed within a Christian context. The strength of this cultural heritage is such that even today, in theory though not in practice, religious education and daily acts of worship are compulsory in schools.

Salvation, morality and right conduct according to the teachings of the Christian churches have been educational goals applicable to all strata of society. Christianity, particularly in its protestant forms, is essentially an intellectual and educational religion, based upon a series of books collected together as the Christian Bible. For centuries readings and texts taken from these books and sermons based upon them, together with the Lord's Prayer, the Ten Commandments, psalms, hymns, images, pictures, the catechism, festivals, feasts, fastings, the calendar of the ecclesiastical year, have shaped, in varying degrees, the lives and learning of the people.

In the eighteenth century the rurally-based rationality of the Anglican Church was challenged and later complemented by the enthusiasm of new dissent, particularly in the shape of Methodism with its great preachers, hymns, class meetings and Sunday schools. A powerful religious dimension thus reached many outposts of industrialising England and Wales, not only the factory workers of the North and Midlands, but even the forgotten tin miners of Cornwall. Radical, secular and working class movements drew upon this Christian ethos, and it has been noted that for every one socialist produced by Karl Marx there have been a hundred produced by the Christian Bible. Nineteenth-century Chartist meetings began with hymn singing, just as twentieth-century cup finals have been preceded by 'Abide with me'.

The religious ideal has often been used as a conservative and stabilising force: intellectually, morally, socially and economically. For centuries the poor have been consoled with the doctrine that it is easier for a camel to pass through the eye of a needle than it is for a rich man to enter into the kingdom of heaven. 'All things bright and beautiful', that most popular of nineteenth-century children's hymns, confirmed the divine right not only of the queen but of the social order in general.

> The rich man in his castle,
> The poor man at his gate,
> God made them, high or lowly,
> And ordered their estate.

New knowledge and values often have been initially proscribed, but subsequently incorporated into the Christian framework. Thus in the early thirteenth century some writings of Aristotle were banned under pain of excommunication for their supposed anti-Christian elements. Subsequently, however, the Thomist or scholastic revolution in thought reconciled Aristotelianism and Christianity on the grounds that 'philosophy examines the natural order by the light of reason: theology, the supernatural order as revealed in the word of God'.[3] Similarly in the nineteenth century new scientific theories, particularly those connected with the origins of the earth and of the human race, were denounced from pulpits throughout the land as being contrary to the accounts of those events as described in the book of *Genesis*.[4] Again an accommodation was found, in the non-literal interpretation of certain sections of the Bible and in the reassertion of the essentially universal (turned towards one God) nature of knowledge.

Though it is dangerous to generalise, it is not difficult to point to tangible evidence of decline in the strength of the Christian ideal in education. In a physical sense the new universities, polytechnics and teacher training institutions of the twentieth century, unlike their precursors in higher education, made little provision for a place of religious worship. Practising Christians (though the term is difficult to define) now probably constitute a smaller proportion of the teaching force than at any time in the last thirteen hundred years. The 1944 Act, however, required compulsory religious education and a daily corporate act of worship.[5] These provisions, though often flouted, reflected a further attempt to use the school to promote the Christian ideal. Christian values and norms, in various disguises, and often based on social rather than religious principles, continue to permeate a predominantly secular society.

Ideal Society

Britain, an outpost on the rim of the known world, was subjected in turn in the post-Roman period to Anglo-Saxon, Danish and Norman invasions. As a consequence its people spoke different languages and dialects, whilst its clergy, who formed a separate estate subject to separate laws and discipline, struggled to preserve as esoteric Latin culture. Occupation of the throne was frequently disputed, and feudal lords, private armies and local justice prevailed in many areas of the country. In the face of starvation, plague, superstition and the other immediate problems of daily life, survival in this world and salvation in the next were the realistic and legitimate goals of a high proportion of the population. In a wider sense too medieval Christendom with its strong sense of sin and unworthiness was suspended uneasily between the dimly glimpsed glories of the Ancient World on the one hand, and the uncertainties of Purgatory, Heaven and Hell on the other.

In the sixteenth century society underwent radical changes. The accession of the Welsh-born Henry Tudor in 1485 brought an end not only to the Wars of the Roses, but also to centuries of strife between England and Wales. The situation was confirmed by parliamentary 'Acts of Union' in 1536 and 1543. The church ceased to exist as a separate entity within the state. Its connections with Rome were broken, much of its property including that of the religious orders was confiscated. A national church, with the sovereign at its head, a new prayer book in English and a summary of doctrine set forth in thirty-nine articles, became the official guardian of education. At the same time the spread of books consequent upon the development of the printing trade, and the influx of humanist ideas, with their emphasis upon achievement in this world rather than the next, encouraged the goal of a more capable, literate, yet still godly commonwealth. Visions of a new society founded upon universal education were particularly manifest in England in the twenty years following 1640. Comenius, Dury, Hartlib and Petty,[6] though critical of much current educational practice, and firm believers in the potential of 'pansophia' (universal knowledge) to regenerate and reform, were not seeking to overturn society as such. 'Levellers' and 'Diggers', however, like Overton and Winstanley, saw education as a prime means of achieving a more radical social transformation.[7]

The restoration of 1660 gave grudging toleration to dissenters. The reality of Catholic reconversion occurred in 1685–8, its ghost appeared briefly to the north in 1715 and 1745.[8] Eighteenth-century society saw government, the professions, and the educational institutions associated with them in the hands of the Anglican Church. Not until the religious census of 1851 did dissent achieve a confidence and recognition in any way commensurate with its support, at that time, of some half of the worshippers in the country.[9]

In the late eighteenth and early nineteenth centuries Christianity in general and the Established Church in particular came under radical attack, epitomised in Tom Paine's[10] *Age of Reason* (1794) and Jeremy Bentham's[11] *Church of Englandism* (1818). Paine's *Rights of Man* (1791) proposed a new basis for English society more akin to those of post revolutionary America and France. Bentham, the classic English *philosophe*, and his disciples, exposed society and its institutions to the light of reason by means of the torch of utility. Robert Owen's *A New View of Society* (1816) found expression at New Lanark and in other more ambitious and high sounding experiments both in the old world and in the new.

Though some institutions which took root at this time, friendly societies, co-operatives and trade unions, were to become integral parts of English society, revolutionary political, social and educational change did not occur. Instead the ideal of society was reformed by parliamentary means. Recognition was given to the wealth, respectability and social and political aspirations of the middling classes. The repeal of the Test and Corporation Acts in 1828, Catholic Emancipation in 1829, the reform of parliamentary and municipal government from 1832 and 1835, and the abolition of the Corn Laws in 1846 gave substance to this new ideal. In consequence its supporters were quite numerous and powerful enough to withstand, even in 1848, the assault of Chartism, that complex, syncretic, political, economic and educational protest movement which flourished in the 1830s and 1840s. Indeed potentially radical educational institutions like the mechanics' institutes, were often the means whereby ambitious members of the lower middle and artisan classes first became associated with the existing local social and political order.

By the mid-nineteenth century the rationalism of the enlightenment, a belief in progress in all things material and moral, the ideas of nationalism and liberalism and the increasing reality of collectivism, combined to produce the ideal of national education. National education, as seen from above, was to encompass the various strata of society, ranging from the great public and proprietary schools at one end of the spectrum, through three grades of endowed schools and a variety of private and elementary establishments to ragged and workhouse schools at the other. The education of males of the upper classes still looked back to the ideal or idealised societies of the Ancient World; in particular to Athens and Rome. Public schools, Oxford and Cambridge Universities and the classical traditions surrounding them played a key role in preserving the aristocratic nature of English government and society; an oligarchy masquerading in the guise of democracy. In the late nineteenth and early twentieth centuries the much vaunted glories of the British Empire and Navy, and the high standards of living relative to other countries, gave all groups in the nation a belief in their own economic, intellectual and moral superiority over foreigners, and over the 'lesser breeds without the law'.[12] In the twentieth century, except during two world wars, England has struggled hard to find an identity. To the outsider, in spite of the ideals of a more caring and egalitarian society, a new artistic excellence, a more popularised culture, all of which have important educational implications, she presents the image of an uncertain and divided country, still fighting the battles of the past rather than the present.

Ideal Men

Plato's ideal human being was the philosopher ruler, male or female, the ultimate product of the educational system set forth in the *Republic* and the *Laws*. Though Aristotle's *Politics* was principally concerned with the good state, the *Ethics* focused rather upon the individual. Since man is distinguished from animals and plants by his reason, it is argued, the good life is that lived in accordance with rational principles. Indeed disinterested intellectual activity is the highest form of human existence. Not all human beings can excel in this sphere, but all can achieve moral excellence. The purpose of education is to bring each individual, through training in good habits and life in a good society, to moral goodness, and to develop in the few the capacity to choose right conduct for themselves and to provide guidance for others. *Pietas, gravitas, humanitas*,[13] ideals from the days of the Roman Republic, have had a particular appeal in English history. In the *Institutio* of Quintilian, the most important educational thinker of the Roman period, as in the writings of Cicero,[14] there was an emphasis on practical statesmanship, with the ideal of the orator rather than the philosopher.

For medieval Europe the concept of the ideal man found expression in the reality of the life lived by Jesus Christ in a subject state during the first century of the Roman Empire. Canonisation of those who most closely approximated to this ideal provided a further series of earthly examples, their virtues extolled in various 'Lives of the Saints'. Heroes of the English church included not only clerics like Augustine and Bede,[15] but also gentle monarchs, St Edmund in the ninth century, St Edward in the eleventh.[16] On the other hand Alfred the Great, like Charlemagne, exemplified the Christian warrior king.[17] The ideal of chivalry, a Western European phenomenon which originated from France, flourished in England from the twelfth century. Its writings were the romances, and later the courtesy books which portrayed the ideal page, squire and knight. The knight in shining armour, brave, courteous, devoted to the service of God and the King, protector of women, defender of the oppressed, became a permanent ideal in English education. Its enduring heroes, however, like St George and King Arthur,[18] were plucked from the reality of their historical contexts.

The ideal of Renaissance man originated in Italian humanism. To the qualities of courtly behaviour and knightly skills were added the accomplishments of the scholar; learning, intelligence and wit. In 1528 the ideal was set forth by Baldassare Castiglione in *The Book of the Courtier*, based upon the example of Frederigo, Duke of Urbino. Three years later appeared *The Boke named the Governour*, probably the first book on education to be printed in English. Sir Thomas Elyot, its author, was a royal secretary and scholar, and symbolised the connection between the new learning and statesmanship also exemplified in the careers of More and Fisher, and in the writings of Ascham, Cleland, Humphrey and Peacham. Henry VIII, influenced no doubt by the *Institutio* of Erasmus,[19] written in 1516 for the benefit of Charles V, prescribed a thoroughly humanist education for his son. Protestant Christian and classical elements were thus combined with traditional outdoor pursuits of riding, hunting and martial exercises, to produce the ideal prince. Skilled tutors, including Cheke and Cox, both Cambridge men, ensured that by the age of fourteen the young King Edward was fluent in Latin and French, and competent in the Greek, Italian and Spanish languages. Amongst classical authors he was familiar with the works of Plato, Aristotle and Cicero. Modern studies included geography, natural philosophy and music.

Such an ideal persisted into the seventeenth century, and was reformulated in *Some Thoughts concerning Education,* first published in 1693, and written for the education of a gentleman's son. John Locke prescribed therein the following order of educational priorities: Virtue, Wisdom, Breeding and Learning. These have been identified with the Christian, Humanist, Courtesy and Rationalist traditions respectively. Though Locke, like Henry VIII and Rousseau, was concerned with the education of individuals through the means of tutors the nineteenth-century public school was an attempt to produce gentlemen in considerable numbers. Thomas Arnold[20] of Rugby was himself a prototype of this God fearing, classically steeped, truth-telling, earnest, breed. Newman provided a similar rationale in *The Idea of a University* (1873) with his defence of liberal as distinct from useful education. Liberal education was designed to produce a healthy mind, and universities were to be essentially places of residence and discussion rather than of research. If any practical end had to be assigned to university studies it was to be the production of good members and leaders of society. The ideal English gentleman was an amateur, above the details of specialised knowledge, industry or trade. He was possessed of sufficient wealth, leisure, moral stature and confidence to play his role in public service, politics and government, or in the public professions — church, law or armed services. The relevance or otherwise of that ideal in the different social, economic, political and international circumstances of twentieth-century Britain, underlies much of the debate about the purpose of education today. Since the Second World War, indeed, the ideal of the gentleman has been seriously challenged, though not yet entirely supplanted by the ideal of the professional. For example even in cricket, that most English of sporting institutions, gentlemen have been abolished, so that all now are merely players.

Good leaders, moreover, presuppose good followers, and in the twentieth century the ideals of 'followership' and service have been strongly challenged, not least in some educational contexts. Throughout the centuries popular culture whilst in part confirming the Christian and gentlemanly ideals has also celebrated such opponents of law and order as Robin Hood, Dick Turpin and the Lincolnshire Poacher. In opposition to the sober, honest, punctual, deferential worker beloved by employers may be placed the widely-held belief that religion is the opium of the people and work the curse of the drinking classes.

Ideal Women

The ideal Spartan woman, like her male counterpart, was to be proficient in a number of skills of service to the state, including physical fitness and fighting. Elsewhere in Ancient Greece in spite of Plato, as in Rome, the female ideal was that of the skilled domestic manager and male helpmeet. Women usually were excluded from intellectual education; a woman's role, in the words of Pericles, was 'not to show more weakness than is natural to her sex', and 'not to be talked about for good or evil among men'.

Christianity has no concept of God the mother, nor of God the daughter, though the Virgin Mary has been venerated as the mother of God and nuns may be considered to be the brides of Christ. Though some females were canonised, women in the Middle Ages were still seen by men as subordinate yet potentially dangerous creatures. In the Old and New Testaments, in the writings of such early fathers as Jerome and Tertullian, and of thirteenth-century Aristotelians like Vincent de Beauvais and Aquinas, women and girls were sources of lust and sin, temptresses with a potential evil influence upon the nobility of man. Their education, therefore was to be neither intellectual nor physical, but essentially moral and social. Aquinas indeed described woman as 'a mutilated man'. The most famous medieval manual of girls education, *The Book of the Knight of La Tour-Landry*, of 1372, extolled the virtues of piety, chastity, modesty and temperance. Submission to husbands was enjoined, 'a woman ought not to strive with her husband, nor give him no displeasure'.[21]

From the later fifteenth century, however, printing and Protestantism were to modify this ideal. Moral education in sixteenth-century England implied some knowledge of the Bible, though a Statute of 1543 originally reserved this to private reading by noblewomen and gentlewomen only. By the seventeenth century some gentlewomen, like their male counterparts, were using shorthand to take down sermons. Sixteenth-century humanism inspired a number of works on the education of gentlewomen, and some highly educated ideal and idealised females, including Lady Jane Grey and Elizabeth Tudor. In spite of such examples, however, the education of women in general remained in the home rather than in the school, and excluded both a study of the classical languages and entry into the political and professional worlds. Though the ideal woman of the period might attain a wider range of accomplishments than her medieval forbears, she was expected to acquire and employ them within the domestic situation. Seventeenth-century reformers, like Comenius, included girls in their plans for universal basic education, but there was no major change in the male view of the female role; Rousseau maintained that 'the whole education of woman should be relative to man'.

A new vision of the ideal woman was provided by Mary Wollstonecraft[22] in *Thoughts on the Education of Daughters* (1786) and *A Vindication of the Rights of Women* (1792). This latter work, her most important, was prompted by Wollstonecraft's dismay that the French Revolution was proclaiming freedom and equality for all men, but not for women. It was male dominated society, she argued, which encouraged women to be petty, timid and helpless creatures. Women were deprived of legal and political rights and denied the education and opportunity to earn an independent livelihood. Wollstonecraft's essential aim was to present women as beings capable of moral responsibility, reason and intellectual growth. Reason, the immortal God-given quality which distinguished the human race from the animals, was bestowed upon males and females alike. In the nineteenth century, however, England indulged in a final orgy of domesticity, presided over by a queen who incongruously condemned 'this mad wicked folly of women's rights'.[23] Gentlewomen in small numbers were admitted to higher education, but not to such established professions as the church and the law, nor to public affairs. As a result teaching became the major employment avenue for educated women, although even in this area they received lower salaries than males until well into the twentieth century. After the First World War those women who during the years of conflict had been employed in traditionally male occupations were ousted from them once again. In 1918 when the first element of women's suffrage was tacked on to a bill to enfranchise all males, the vote was restricted to women over 30 who were householders or wives of householders. Not until 1928 did women have a vote in their own right on the same terms as men, not until 1970 was the general principle of equal pay for equal work established by statute.

The differing concepts of the ideal man and the ideal woman have been a fundamental feature both of English history and of English education. The campaign against sex-role typing in education continues, and the right to determine the concept of the ideal woman is still being wrested by women from men. By 1979 England and Wales could countenance both a female monarch and a female prime minister, but not yet a female archbishop or cardinal, nor even a female parish priest.

Childhood and Adolescence

Ideas about childhood and adolescence have changed significantly over the centuries. At one extreme children have been seen as innately wicked, beings to be purged with the greatest possible speed of those imperfections which inhibit the attainment of adulthood. At the other extreme children have been considered as essentially good, with childhood and adolescence recognised as separate stages of great intrinsic worth and particularly suitable for schooling and other means of education.

It has been suggested that in the medieval period as soon as children were weaned away from their mothers they became a part of adult society. As infants, so susceptible to disease and death, they were of little account. Once they became newly recruited and imperfect members of that society they were dressed and pictorially represented as miniature adults. From the age of about seven, and precision in these matters must have been rare, they could be schooled, worked, married, imprisoned and hanged. Schoolrooms might contain children and young persons of all ages, and the terms *pueri* and *adolescentes*[24] were indiscriminately used.

At the same time there were recognised gradations. The several ages of man, most frequently three, seven or twelve, were a constant theme of later medieval literature. These were drawn from a variety of sources: classical antiquity, the seasons, the signs of the zodiac. Apprenticeship, knighthood and university degrees all required fixed periods of training and study.

These patterns of society were changed with the ending of feudalism and of traditional apprenticeship. In the rapidly growing towns of the late eighteenth and early nineteenth century many adolescents acquired an economic independence which made possible both geographical and social mobility and early marriage. Robert Owen who started work at the age of ten became manager of a cotton mill at the age of nineteen and a part owner by the time he was twenty-eight.

Since the seventeenth century, however, a different ideal of childhood and adolescence had been developed. Comenius, the Czech educator whose wanderings in exile included a sojourn in England in 1641–2, advocated a full education for every child to the age of twelve, irrespective of sex, class, ability or race. Universal education in infancy and childhood, however, was for Comenius but a beginning. He also envisaged two further six year stages of adolescent preparation for adult life which would be made available to all who could profit thereby.

Locke prescribed a mixture of kindness and good sense in the upbringing of the young. Like Comenius he wished learning to be made rational, purposeful and attractive. He showed respect for the natural state of childhood, 'it must be permitted children not only to divert themselves, but to do it after their own fashion, provided it be innocently and without prejudice to their health', or '... the chief art is to make all that they have to do sport and play too'.

Rousseau in *Emile* extended infancy and childhood until 15 years of age, with a further five years of adolescence to follow. For the first twelve years he urged a policy of non-intervention: 'Leave childhood to ripen in your children. In a word, beware of giving anything they need today, if it can be deferred without danger till tomorrow'.

This romantic view of the natural goodness of the child was in stark contrast to that of the imperfect adult. It found an eloquent and lasting expression in English literature in the poetry of Blake, Coleridge and Wordsworth. Similarly Dickens made children and childhood a central theme in the English novel.[25]

Concepts of childhood, adolescence and natural growth became an essential part both of the doctrine of age-specific, compulsory schooling and of the modern progressive educational tradition as expressed in the writings of Froebel, Montessori, Dewey, Isaacs and Piaget.[26] Child development became the key component of English teacher training colleges in the middle years of the twentieth century. The Plowden Report of 1967 was entitled *Children and their Primary Schools*. The concept of adolescence was a justification for compulsory secondary schooling.

The Literate Ideal

It is customary to write the history of education in terms of the growth of a literate culture. Indeed universal literacy is a fundamental goal of the schooled society of the nineteenth and twentieth centuries. It is difficult to assign a starting point to this process, but the medieval period furnished two important developments: those from 'memory to written record' and from 'script to print'.[27]

Thus from the Norman Conquest of 1066 there was an increasing supply of documents written in Latin. The twelfth and thirteenth centuries, indeed, witnessed a veritable document explosion. Charters, letters, accounts, a variety of legal records, registers, learned and literary works proliferated. From the sixteenth century the introduction of the printed page was consolidated by the widespread use of the English Bible and prayerbook.

There are, however, varying notions and degrees of literacy, semi-literacy and illiteracy, and non-literate culture (a culture not based upon the written word) also has an essential place in the history of English education. The ideal of a mass reading and writing public with universally high standards of literacy is a very modern phenomenon. The realistic purpose of mass instruction under the protestant ethos was to develop the mastery of reading a limited number of religious works. During the nineteenth century national education broadened the number and scope of such texts, but the ideal of universal and indiscriminate reading and writing for meaning is essentially a twentieth-century goal.

Today's popular newspapers rely heavily upon banner headlines, provocative photographs, human interest stories, sport and advertisements. Films, radio and television have been the significant new developments in twentieth-century culture. Each provides entertainment and information, a means of communication, and a potential art form. The Open University[28] affords the clearest link between the formal educational system and the new media. Modern methods of storage and retrieval ensure that this audio-visual material will become as much a part of historical evidence as the written record.

Non-literate culture from the past has been more difficult to define and to assess. For example there is scant record of the non-literate culture of the medieval period with its roots in memory, tradition and learning by heart. We do not know to what extent ordinary people had some facility in more than one spoken language or dialect whether English, Welsh, French or Latin. Were they indeed more educated in this sense than the cloistered monk, poring for a whole year over his single book? Oral practices have remained at the heart of many aspects of religious and temporal culture, for example the marriage service and the court of law. In the middle ages the testimony of twelve good men and true might well have been preferred to that of written documentation so susceptible to forgery, emendation or unavailability. Oral methods of teaching have persisted to the present day in all levels of education. The literate ideal, if interpreted as universal adult ability to read and understand any written material, has never yet been achieved in English history.

The Universal Ideal

The history of English education reveals a variety of ideals and aims: explicit and implicit, extrinsic and intrinsic, intellectual and moral, secular and religious, individual and societal. In most periods of time it has been possible to relate educational aims to particular groups in society: rulers, fighting men, clerics, merchants, craftsmen, labourers, women, and so on. The term education might be applied to the process whereby a society or state seeks to furnish itself with wise rulers, brave warriors, holy clerics, efficient businessmen, industrious workers, and domesticated womenfolk. Though most social systems are conservative and tend towards social stratification, some social mobility has always been possible in English society, and education has been a key means of supplying it. In a society with any meritocratic dimensions education can serve to produce, identify and select individuals according to ability.

The ideal of universal education has often coexisted with the reality of education according to one's station.

From the medieval period onwards the universal ideal could be expressed in Christian terms. All children and adults were potentially equal in the sight of God, all had souls to be saved, all therefore should be instructed in the basic tenets of the faith. From the sixteenth century protestantism laid a further emphasis upon the universal ability to read the Bible.

By the later nineteenth century, however, the universal educational ideal had found a new form. This owed much to the rationalism of the later eighteenth century and more to the romanticism of the early nineteenth. It envisaged a wider range of educational objectives, temporal and spiritual, though as reduced to its lowest common denominator, the 'four Rs' of the elementary school curriculum, reading, writing, arithmetic and religion, it seemed limited enough. This particular universal ideal has been both the cause and the consequence of modern state intervention in education, and compulsory school attendance its most distinctive feature. The tutelary state has assumed the role of surrogate parent. In so doing a large 'schooling' interest has been created, teachers, academics, administrators and the like, committed to this particular method of defining and achieving the universal educational ideal. Schooling has thus become virtually compulsory for all between the ages of five and sixteen.

Compulsory schooling of the young is the classic modern expression of the universal ideal and has so far survived a wide range of critics, including freeschoolers like the Russells and A.S. Neill,[29] and deschoolers like Reimer and Illich.[30] Indeed in the twentieth century the universal ideal has been significantly extended. The school-leaving age has been steadily raised, in 1918 to fourteen, in 1947 to fifteen, and to sixteen in 1972. Since the Second World War provision has been made for an increasing proportion of young people and adults to engage in further and higher education. Nevertheless this proportion is still low in comparison with those of the USA and many European countries. Access is restricted by means of qualification and competition, whilst the scheme for compulsory part-time education to eighteen, envisaged as long ago as 1918, has not been implemented.

Finally, more emphasis has been placed in the last thirty years upon the egalitarian dimensions of the universal educational ideal. Few now believe in the eighteenth-century ideal of absolute equality of attainment. Few now share the earlier twentieth-century belief that children are possessed of a fixed and measurable quotient of innate intelligence. Instead the emphasis has been placed upon ensuring greater equality of educational opportunity, most recently with the introduction of the comprehensive secondary school. This has even led to the doctrine of positive discrimination in favour of the disadvantaged, in the case of special grants for schools in educational priority areas, or special arrangements by Oxford and Cambridge colleges for pupils from comprehensive schools.

The contemporary ideal of universal education through the medium of mass schooling was formulated in the nineteenth century. Its noblest expression was in the words of Matthew

Arnold, scholar, poet, school inspector and friend of children.

> Plenty of people will try to indoctrinate the masses with the set of
> ideas and judgements constituting the creed of their own profession
> or party. Our religious and political organisations give an example of
> this way of working on the masses. I condemn neither way; but
> culture works differently. It does not try to teach down to the level of
> inferior classes; it does not try to win them for this or that sect of its
> own, with ready-made judgements and watch-words. It seeks to do
> away with classes; to make the best that has been thought and known
> in the world current everywhere ...
>
> This is the *social idea;* and the men of culture are the true apostles
> of equality. The great men of culture are those who have had a
> passion for diffusing, for making prevail, for carrying from one end
> of society to the other, the best knowledge, the best ideas of their
> time; who have laboured to divest knowledge of all that was harsh,
> uncouth, difficult, abstract, professional, exclusive; to humanise it,
> to make it efficient outside the clique of the cultivated and learned,
> yet still remaining the *best* knowledge and thought of the time ...[31]

Conclusion

Matthew Arnold's words are themselves a fitting conclusion to this
section; a reaffirmation of human concern with matters of value and
worth. There has been a broad consensus that education is a prime
agent in increasing culture and civilisation and in diminishing
anarchy and barbarism.

Nevertheless the history of education expressed as a history of
ideas and ideals has also been a history of conflict, contest and
grudging accommodation. Religion and reason have been uneasy
bedfellows. So too have excellence and equality (the latter itself at
odds over the issue of equality of opportunity versus equality of
attainment). These are not purely esoteric disputes. For example
the recurring theme of conflict between 'traditional' and 'progressive' educators in large part reflects similar conflicts in the
wider worlds of social and political ideas and ideals.

NOTES

1 **Plato** (427–347 BC) and **Aristotle** (384–322 BC) the greatest

philosophers of Ancient Greece; **St Augustine** of Hippo (353–430) and **St Thomas Aquinas** (1226–74) who exemplified the Christian thought of the early and later Middle Ages; **John Amos Comenius** (1592–1670) the Czech pastor, philologist and educational writer; **John Henry Newman** (1801–90) the Anglican divine who became a cardinal in the Roman Catholic church; **John Dewey** (1859–1952) the American pragmatic philosopher and educationist.

2 For definitions of education including that of initiation *see* R.S. Peters, *Ethics and Education* (1966), Chapter 2.

3 **M. Deanesly**, *A History of the Medieval Church 590–1500* (1951), p. 175. **Thomist**, pertaining to St Thomas Aquinas.

4 A controversy centred around *The Origin of Species* (1859) written by the naturalist Charles Darwin (1809–92).

5 **R.A. Butler** (b.1902) was president of the Board of Education at the time of the Education Act of 1944. The school day was to begin with a corporate act of worship. Religious instruction in local authority schools was to be given in accordance with a syllabus agreed by representatives of the religious denominations.

6 **John Dury** (1596–1680), **Samuel Hartlib** (1600–62) and **William Petty** (1623–87) were amongst the leading educational reformers and writers of their day. The much travelled Comenius came to England in 1641.

7 **The Levellers** were a democratic group which flourished in the parliamentary army during the later 1640s. **The Diggers** sought in particular to promote economic and social equality by cultivating untilled land.

8 During his brief reign 1685–8, James II (1633–1701) encouraged the spread of Roman Catholicism. In 1715 his son James Edward (1688–1766) the 'Old Pretender' failed to regain the throne. In 1745 his grandson Charles Edward (1720–88) the 'Young Pretender' was similarly unsuccessful. Both attempts began with landings in Scotland.

9 **The Religious Census** taken in 1851 seemed to show that the Anglican Church no longer had an absolute majority of worshippers.

10 **Thomas Paine** (1737–1809), the radical political writer who though born in England spent much of his adult life in revolutionary America and France.

11 **Jeremy Bentham** (1748–1832), philosopher and legal reformer. His application of the principle of utilitarianism, 'of what use is it?', had much in common with the principles of the *philosophes* of the eighteenth-century French enlightenment.

12 The phrase of Rudyard Kipling (1865–1936), who himself born in Bombay, captured the essential spirit of British Imperialism.

13 'Piety', 'gravity' and 'humanity', though the nearest English equivalents lack the force of the Latin originals.

14 **Cicero** (106–43 BC), **Quintilian** (c. 35–95 AD).

15 In 597 **St Augustine of Canterbury** (d.c. 605 AD), brought Christianity to Kent from Rome. **The Venerable Bede** (673–735 AD), scholar and historian, was prior of the monastery at Jarrow in Northumbria.

16 **Edmund, King of East Anglia** 855–70, martyred by the Danes. **Edward the Confessor** (c. 1004–1066), founder of Westminster Abbey.

17 **Alfred the Great** (849–99), King of Wessex who defeated the Danes. **Charlemagne** (742–814), King of the Franks who defeated the Saxons, Lombards, Saracens and Magyars and who in 800 was crowned as emperor in Rome.

18 **St George,** patron saint of England from 1349 was probably a Christian soldier martyred by Diocletian in Nicomedia on 23 April 303. **King Arthur** (c.600) was a fabled Celtic warrior. According to legend, **St David** (d.c. 589), patron saint of Wales, was a grandson of Arthur's uncle.

19 **Desiderius Erasmus** (1466–1536), Dutch Renaissance humanist who spent many years in England.

20 **Thomas Arnold** (1795–1842), headmaster of Rugby School, 1828–42.

21 **Sylvester** (1970), p. 45.

22 **Mary Wollstonecraft** (1759–97), wife of William Godwin and mother of Mary Shelley.

23 **Victoria** (1819–1901), Queen from 1837 who nevertheless sought to exercise considerable influence upon the choice of ministers and the conduct of foreign affairs.

24 *Pueri* — children (usually boys) up to the age of 17; *adolescentes* — young persons between the ages of 15 and 30.

25 *Oliver Twist* (1838) was his second book. *See* P. Collins, *Dickens and Education* (1965).

26 **Friedrich Froebel** (1782–1852), German educational reformer and founder of the kindergarten movement; **Maria Montessori** (1870–1952), Italian doctor and designer of didactic materials to promote sensory development; **Susan Isaacs** (1885–1948), whose work at the Malting House School and the London Institute of Education provided a scientific analysis of the intellectual growth and social development of young children; **Jean Piaget** (1896–1980) the influential Swiss developmental psychologist.

27 **M.T. Clanchy,** *From Memory to Written Record: England 1066–1307* (1979), H.J. Chaytor, *From Script to Print* (1945).

28 **The Open University** whose first students were enrolled in 1970, makes full use of radio and television programmes and materials sent through the post.

29 **Bertrand Russell** (1872–1970) and his wife, Dora, founders of Beacon Hill School; **A.S. Neill** (1883–1973), founder of Summerhill School.

30 **I.D. Illich,** *Deschooling Society* (1971); E. Reimer, *School is Dead* (1971).
31 **M. Arnold,** *Culture and Anarchy* (1869), Chapter 1.

3 Organisation and Control of Education

Three of the many historical dimensions of the complex structure of formal education are examined in this chapter. The first summarises the roles of major controlling bodies; churches, central and local government. The second focuses upon teachers, the key personnel in the educational process. The third considers the role of examinations, a central feature of the modern system.

The Churches

Church control of education has been a basic feature of English history.

In the medieval period the Catholic Church exercised this control through various bodies: bishops and cathedral chapters, collegiate churches and monastic orders. From the sixteenth century a new power, that of the Anglican Church, predominated in the universities and grammar schools of England. This Church survived two major challenges. Roman Catholicism was restored during the reign of Mary Tudor, 1553–8. Puritanism was in the ascendancy during the years of the Civil War and the Interregnum, 1640–60.

The year 1660, however, produced a restoration of monarchy, parliament and established Church which has survived until the present day. An Act of Uniformity of 1662 required clergy, dons, tutors and schoolmasters to be in conformity with Anglican liturgy and to be licensed by a bishop. Anglican control of grammar schools and universities continued well into the second half of the nineteenth century. Clerical headmasters were the ideal, complemented at Oxford and Cambridge by bachelor dons in holy orders. Only Anglicans could be admitted to degrees. In the first half of the nineteenth century the majority of such graduates themselves proceeded into the Church. Nonconformity, however, had by this time established a permanent, albeit subordinate, place in English and Welsh society. In 1689 an Act of Toleration gave freedom of worship to most Protestant nonconformists, whilst penalties against unlicensed teaching were less strictly enforced. In 1700 the judgement in Cox's case exempted all but teachers in grammar schools from the necessity of a bishop's licence.[1] By this date the Presbyterian Fund (1689) and the Congregational Fund Board (1695), had provided the basis for the education and training of a Dissenting ministry.

The Charity schools which flourished in the early eighteenth century were encouraged and to some extent co-ordinated, if not always controlled, by the Society for Promoting Christian Knowledge, an Anglican body established by 1699. Sunday schools were essentially, though not invariably, under religious control, and in 1835 the Sunday School Union claimed over 900,000 scholars. By 1851 there were over two million enrolments in Sunday schools.[2]

The British and Foreign School Society, founded originally in 1808 as the Royal Lancasterian Society, was, like the Sunday School Union, non-denominational in character. Nineteenth-century elementary education prior to 1870, however, was in the main controlled and supplied by denominationally based organisations. Chief amongst these was the National Society for Promoting the Education of the Poor in the Principles of the Established Church, set up in 1811 under the chairmanship of the Archbishop of Canterbury. Others included the Wesleyan Education Committee and the Catholic Poor School Committee. These four bodies all came to accept government financial assistance, and in consequence by the 1840s were submitting aided schools to government inspection. On the other hand the extreme Voluntaryists, who by 1851 boasted some 364 schools and Homerton training college, were supported by Congregationalists and Baptists and refused government aid and intervention until 1867.[3] Of the 8,000 state-aided elementary schools in England and Wales on the eve of the Education Act of 1870, some 6,000 were National schools, and a further 1,500 British or Wesleyan.[4]

In 1870 elementary schools controlled by the voluntary societies were the best in the country; by 1902 many were in dire straits, having frequently been 'overmatched' by those of the school boards.[5] In consequence the 1902 Act gave voluntary or 'non-provided' schools, as they were to be known, a more secure financial footing. Provision and repair of school buildings remained the responsibility of the denominations, all other costs were to be met from public funds. In return local education authorities (LEAs) were to receive minority representation on the managing bodies of such schools.

In the 1920s and 30s the Board of Education 'black list' of schools in defective premises included twice as many 'non-provided' as provided schools. The 1944 Act accordingly gave buildings and repair grants of up to 50 per cent to 'Voluntary aided' schools. In 1959 these grants were increased to 75 per cent and by 1975 to 85 per cent. Many Anglican schools, however, gave up the unequal struggle and opted for 'Controlled' status, whereby though the Church authorities retained ownership in principle, they could appoint only one-third of the managers, and schools would be financed and maintained as if they were council schools.

Thus in the first half of the twentieth century, as the following table shows, perhaps for the first time in over a thousand years, the Churches became junior partners in the control of schools and of their teachers. Moreover Anglican predominance in such voluntary schooling as does exist is more seriously challenged than it has been since the seventeenth century.

Percentages of children on rolls of schools in England and Wales (omitting independent, nursery and special schools)[6]

Type of school	1900	1938	1962
Council	47.0	69.6	77.6
Church of England	40.2	22.1	11.9
Roman Catholic	5.4	7.4	8.4
Other	7.4	0.9	2.1

Central Government

Central government interest can be traced back to individual kings from the early medieval period, for example both Alfred in the ninth century and Edgar in the tenth actively encouraged the development of education. The king's government was a major employer of educated labour, particularly with the rapid development of written records from the twelfth century. Similarly in the first decade of the fifteenth century Owen Glendower, self proclaimed prince, sought to establish two new universities, one in the north and one in the south of an independent Wales, primarily as a source of well-educated administrators.

Universities appear to have been particularly susceptible to royal control and influence. The tradition that Oxford University was founded by Alfred may be completely discounted, but its early development could well have been assisted in the 1160s by Henry II's edict recalling scholars from abroad. In 1265 Henry III suppressed a nascent university at Northampton, founded by migrations from Oxford and Cambridge, whilst in 1334, again at the request of the Oxford authorities, Edward III similarly ensured that another incipient university at Stamford was put down.

Kings in parliament legislated for the control of apprenticeship, though a statute of 1406 in the reign of Henry IV had wider educational implications. It sought to prevent the children of poor labourers from being apprenticed to a craft, 'Provided Always, that every Man or Woman, of what Estate or Condition that he be, shall be free to set their Son or Daughter to take Learning at any manner School that pleaseth them within the Realm'.[7]

In the 1530s Henry VIII, with parliamentary approval, made himself head of the Church in England and Wales. Central government control over matters religious and educational was shown in the suppression of monasteries and nunneries and the confiscation of their property. Eight former monastic cathedrals were reconstituted, the majority with a new 'King's' grammar school. Legislation of Edward VI's reign which saw the final suppression of colleges of priests, chantries and religious gilds would have had more serious educational consequences had not determined efforts been made to preserve most of the schools connected with such bodies. Between 1549 and 1559 the universities were subjected to three series of royal visitations to establish, disestablish and re-establish the new faith. In 1546 Henry VIII founded Trinity College, Cambridge, and reconstituted Christ Church, Oxford. In the 1540s Regius professorships, to be held as crown appointments, were established at both universities. In 1540 Henry VIII by royal proclamation prescribed the use of but one Latin grammar in schools, that originally compiled by Colet, Lily[8] and Erasmus. This *Royal Grammar,* transmuted in 1758 into the *Eton Latin Grammar,* remained the standard work until the introduction of Kennedy's *Latin Primer* in 1866.

In 1559 Elizabeth I issued royal injunctions which prescribed the continued use of the *Royal Grammar,* and forbade any to teach without the bishop's licence. From 1604 all candidates for the licence were required to submit to the royal supremacy, a test which had been applied to university graduates from 1563.

From the sixteenth century the universities served as places of education for significant numbers of the upper and aspiring ranks of society, and for the clergy, and as places of employment for some of the ablest minds of the age. For the next two centuries central government control of these institutions was seen as an essential means of securing religious and political orthodoxy throughout the land. The dangers were real enough. Roman Catholics in the reign of Elizabeth might see the Queen merely as the bastard daughter of Anne Boleyn. Puritans in the mid-seventeenth century might subscribe to the doctrine of no bishop and no king. Later in the century Whigs and Tories would be aligned with rival houses and factions within them. Not until the second half of the eighteenth century was the protestant Hanoverian succession finally assured.

The relationship between central government and the universities has been a complex one. From 1604 the English universities were each entitled to send members to Parliament, a privilege extended to London in 1871, and to other universities from 1918 until its discontinuance in 1948. Oxford was reformed by the former president of St John's College, William Laud,[9] who in the 1630s became not only Chancellor of the University, and of Trinity College Dublin (founded in 1591 and granted parliamentary representation in 1613), but also Archbishop of Canterbury and a trusted adviser of Charles I. The Laudian statutes of 1636, like the Cambridge statutes of 1570, gave formal power to the meeting of college heads, known at Oxford as the Hebdomadal Board. Congregation and Convocation continued to give an appearance of democracy, but effective power now rested with this conservative oligarchy until the reforms of 1854. The appointment of heads of colleges with a firm commitment to absolute monarchy and to Arminian theology, men with no Papist or puritanical connections, further increased the political subservience of the university. Laud's policies emphasised the functions of the universities as training grounds for orthodox and learned parish clergy. Laudian regulations expressed strong disapproval of the longhaired, high booted, silver spurred, aristocratic undergraduate mentality, and of such activities as poaching, dicing, carousing and wenching. Orthodoxy flourished and Oxford became the centre of the royal cause during the civil war, one of the first of its many lost causes. Though the leaders of the parliamentary side, men such as Pym, Hampden and Cromwell[10] had been university educated, their studies had taken place prior to the scholastic and conservative restoration which reached a peak in the 1630s.

Oxford survived the interregnum under Cromwell's protection, though both universities were subjected to even stricter religious and moral control than in the Laudian period. In 1681 Charles II summoned parliament to Oxford rather than to Westminster. Oxford was particularly affected by the Catholic policies of James II, whilst the accession of the Calvinist William III in 1688 led to more expulsions at Cambridge of those dons, the 'non jurors', who refused to recognise his right to the throne. With the advent of party politics the fortunes of Oxford became linked with those of the high Tories during the reign of Anne, and consequently declined with the accession of George I in 1714. Cambridge was preferred by Hanoverian ministers, particularly the Duke of Newcastle, who became chancellor in 1748. General schemes to cement an alliance between Whig politics and the universities came to nothing, but college elections frequently exhibited a party political dimension. In 1760 Tory Oxford breathed more easily with the accession of George III. Lord North was elected chancellor and the tradition of loyalty to the crown became of greater significance than that of loyalty to the House of Stuart.

Central government intervention in education, therefore, began long before the £20,000 grant for building elementary schools of 1833. In 1839, however, a Committee of the Privy Council on Education was established, presided over by the Lord President. It was originally composed of five ministers including the Chancellor of the Exchequer and Home Secretary. Lord John Russell's immediate concern in establishing the Committee was to increase the numbers and improve the quality of the teaching force. The Committee's brief was to control 'the application of any sums which may be voted by Parliament for the purposes of Education in England and Wales'.[11] Its first and most famous secretary was Dr James Kay (later Kay-Shuttleworth).[12] In 1841 its first inspectors, Rev. John Allen, lecturer in mathematics and chaplain at King's College, London, and the barrister Hugh Tremenheere were given permanent status at salaries of £600 per annum. In 1858 there were 30 inspectors, 16 assistant inspectors, and an annual grant of £836,920. By 1860 the Education Department with an establishment of 127 had become one of the largest civil offices of state.[13]

In 1853 a Department of Science and Art was set up at South Kensington, a direct outcome of the Great Exhibition of 1851. Its purpose was not primary or general education, but rather to instruct the industrial classes in 'secondary' subjects in the fields of science and art. Though begun under the Board of Trade, in 1857 it was placed under the direction of the Education Department with whom it enjoyed an uneasy relationship until the end of the century. From 1856 the Education Department was represented in the House of Commons by a Vice President of the Committee of Council.[14] In the middle of the nineteenth century the central government, through the medium of royal commissions, surveyed the major part of the formal educational landscape. Reports upon the universities in 1852-3 led to Acts for Oxford in 1854 and Cambridge in 1856. Between 1858 and 1861 elementary education was examined by the Newcastle Commissioners. Their report led firstly to the Revised Code of 1862, and ultimately to the Elementary Education Act of 1870. The Clarendon Commission reported in 1864 on nine great public schools, and was followed by a Public Schools Act in 1868. The Taunton Commission, established in 1864 to inquire into all schools not covered by Newcastle and Clarendon, reported in 1868 and was followed by an Endowed Schools Act in the following year.

Sir John Pakington, Conservative MP for Droitwich, was the principal parliamentary advocate of government intervention in education during this crucial mid-nineteenth century period. Though his education bills of 1855 and 1857 were unsuccessful, Pakington's campaign prompted the establishment of the Vice Presidency in 1856 and of the Newcastle Commission in 1858. His Select Committee of 1865-6, of which Bruce, the then Vice President, and Forster were members, revealed the inefficiencies of the Privy Council system. In 1868 the Conservative government introduced an unsuccessful bill to provide for a Minister of Education. In 1870 only Pakington's anxiety about the possible defeat of Forster's Elementary Education Bill prevented his moving an amendment for a Minister and Ministry of Education.

In 1870 indeed the central government was bypassed in the task of filling up the gaps in elementary school provision. New local bodies were created instead. Central government involvement, however, continued much as before. Royal Commissions reported in 1875 on Scientific Instruction (Devonshire), in 1884 on Technical Instruction (Samuelson), in 1888 on Elementary Education (Cross) and 1895 on Secondary Education (Bryce). There was further legislation in the elementary sphere. Compulsory schooling until fourteen though with exemptions from ten was introduced in 1880, most fees were abolished in 1891. The curriculum was influenced by major modifications of the Code. Grants for 'class' subjects were introduced in 1875, whilst the number of grant earning 'specific' subjects begun in 1867 was steadily increased.[15]

In 1899 a Board of Education was established which subsumed the powers of the Education Department, the Science and Art Department and the educational work of the Charity Commissioners. The new board was to consist of a President, the Lord President of the Council, and other ministers including the Chancellor of the Exchequer. In fact it became a fiction and never met. The new body was charged only with 'the superintendence of matters relating to education in England and Wales', and it was widely assumed that no politician of real ability would ever wish to be President of the Board of Education. The Act also established a Consultative Committee.

In 1903 Robert Morant, who from 1895–9 had been assistant director to Michael Sadler at the Department of Special Inquiries and Reports on Education, became secretary to the Board. Though Morant chafed at the Board's limited powers, the principle of control through grants was now applied to the secondary school. Regulations of 1904 prescribed both the subjects to be studied and the minimum hours to be accorded to them. Departmental work was rationalised and separate branches created to deal with elementary, secondary and technical education. A Medical branch was established in 1907 and a Universities branch in 1910 (replaced in 1919 by the University Grants Committee). The Fisher Education Act of 1918 (the historian H.A.L. Fisher was President of the Board of Education in the wartime coalition), promised to establish a truly national system of education. At least half the costs of schooling were to be met from central government funds. Though the Board was now given the power to 'require' LEAs to submit their educational schemes for approval, in the post-war atmosphere of unemployment and financial crisis the law was simply disregarded. In the inter-war period, however, the Board's Consultative Committee came into its own with the great series of Hadow reports.

Central government was galvanised into unprecedented activity by a second World War, 1939–45. In 1941 a 'Green Book' containing a digest of educational reforms proposed during the preceding twenty-five years was circulated 'in a blaze of secrecy' to interested organisations for comment. Its proposals were embodied into an Education bill, which, skilfully guided by the President, R.A. Butler, became law in August 1944. At last a Ministry of Education was created. The Minister's duty was 'to promote the education of the people of England and Wales ... and to secure the effective execution by local authorities, under his control and direction, of the national policy of providing a varied and comprehensive educational service in every area'.[16] In 1964 the Ministry was renamed the Department of Education and Science.

Central Advisory Councils for Education were created, including one for England and one for Wales, and were responsible for much of the educational fact-finding of the post war period. English reports included those in 1959 of Crowther on the education of 15–18 year olds, in 1963 of Newsom on 13–16 year olds of average or less than average ability, and in 1967 of Plowden on primary schools. Welsh reports covered technical education in 1961 and primary education in 1968. These and other surveys, notably that of the Robbins committee on higher education in 1963, prompted the unprecedented growth in public expenditure which occurred during the 1960s. The proportion of national resources committed to education virtually doubled, to well over 6 per cent by the end of the decade, and more than 7 per cent in 1977–8. This growth policy continued with the White Paper of 1972 entitled *Education : A Framework for Expansion*. Ten years later, in the context of recession, unemployment and declining school rolls, central government intervention and control in education is less concerned with expansion and more with cost-effectiveness, accountability and standards. James Callaghan's speech at Ruskin College, Oxford in 1976 and the Green Paper *Education in Schools* of the following year, exemplified a concern for a basic curriculum and more universal standards. An Assessment of Performance Unit (APU) was set up at the DES in 1974. Circular 14/77 sought precise information from LEAs about their curriculum arrangements. The consultative document *A Framework for the School Curriculum* published in 1980 indicated the determination of central government to give a stronger lead in curriculum planning once again.

The limitations of central government's control of education have been shown in the issue of secondary school reorganisation. In the famous Circular 10/65 Anthony Crosland, minister in a Labour government with the declared aim of ending selection at eleven plus in secondary education, did no more than 'request' local authorities to submit plans for comprehensive reorganisation. Though twelve months were given for reply, in 1969, four years later, eighteen authorities had either not responded or had deliberately refused to submit schemes. In 1970 Circular 10/65 was withdrawn by a

Conservative government, and though an Education Act of 1976 was introduced to compel LEAs to go comprehensive, in 1982 grammar schools, and selection for them, still remained. The wider issue of separatism in secondary, and for that matter primary education, as presented by the existence of an independent private, preparatory and public schools system, has as yet remained largely outside central government control.

Local Government

In the medieval period the mayor and burgesses of a town where there was no benefactor, bishop, great church or other religious body to provide a school might themselves shoulder this responsibility. Various inducements could be offered to attract a master: a monopoly of teaching, a salary or livery, a house or schoolroom.

The suppression of monasteries, chantries and religious gilds at the time of the Reformation had important implications for school provision and control. From the 1550s more town corporations assumed responsibility for grammar schools, sometimes by securing a charter, statute or letters patent. At Birmingham and Shrewsbury grants of recently nationalised Church property were obtained to support schools, at Beverley and Hull they were not. Grammar schools already under the control of town corporations, as at Bristol and Nottingham, survived the Edwardian dissolutions intact.

In the seventeenth and eighteenth centuries agencies of local government — town corporations, parish authorities and overseers of the poor — played a part in the provision and control of charity and elementary schooling.

Municipal corporation reform in 1835 encouraged the belief that elementary education should be placed under municipal control. From the 1830s Manchester was the focal point of this movement which culminated in the 1850s with the National Public School Association and a series of unsuccessful bills based on the principle of rate aided education. By the 1860s initiative was passing to Birmingham and the National Education League. By the Elementary Education Act of 1870 responsibility for filling up the gaps in school provision, after the period of grace allotted to the voluntary bodies, was accorded to the newly created School Boards. These *ad hoc* bodies, directly elected and independent of existing forms of local government, were by the end of the nineteenth century controlling the elementary schooling and employing the teachers of nearly half of the children in the country.

School boards ranged in size from that of London (the exception with some fifty members, and with more than half a million pupils) to rural boards with but one school under their control. Boards consisted of between five and fifteen members, elected triennially by the ratepayers. They were frequently the stage for political and religious rivalry, and provided an important political apprenticeship for emergent groups in society, including women and the Independent Labour Party. School boards had considerable powers in such matters as attendance and religious teaching. Though it was generally considered that secondary and adult education, including teacher training, lay outside their control, advanced work was provided in higher grade schools and classes and in evening work.

In 1887 the National Association for the Promotion of Technical Education was formed. An Act of 1889 enabled the newly formed local authorities — county councils, county boroughs and urban sanitary authorities — to raise up to a penny rate for the purposes of technical education, and to create technical instruction committees to supervise this work. From 1890 the so-called 'whisky money', raised from a duty on spirits and beer, could also be applied for this purpose. In the first year £700,000 was made available, and in the financial year ending March 1900 over £1 million was paid to English and Welsh authorities. Such sums were greater than the total expenditure of the Science and Art Department at that time. Control of these funds gave local bodies, particularly the county councils, useful experience in the management of education.

The Education Act of 1902 effected a radical change in the nature and extent of local control. School boards were abolished. The new local education authorities had a duty to ensure the adequate supply of elementary education. They were also to 'consider the educational needs of their area and take such steps as seem to them desirable, to supply or aid the supply of education other than elementary, and to promote the general co-ordination of all forms of education'.[17] This could include the provision of secondary schools and teacher training colleges. Thus some 2,568 school boards and 14,238 bodies of school managers were replaced by 318 Local Education Authorities comprising 63 county councils, 82 county boroughs, and 173 non-county boroughs and urban districts.[18] In many cases the personnel of the former board or technical instruction committee continued to serve under the new authority.

At Leicester, for example, the new education committee consisted of the mayor, twenty-one members of the town council and nine co-opted members, seven of whom were former members of the school board. The clerk to the board became the secretary to the education committee.[19]

Legislation of 1906 and 1907 permitted local authority expenditure on meals and medicals, and the range of ancillary services and activities was further increased under the 1918 Act. It also provided for at least 50 per cent of expenditure to be met from central government funds. This was of particular assistance to London where in 1914, 73 per cent of educational costs were met from rates, as compared with 53 per cent in the rest of England and Wales.[20] Before 1919 each LEA decided its own salary scales for teachers. In that year the first Burnham Committee was established to consider the remuneration of teachers in public elementary schools. In 1921 the first national salary scales for teachers in elementary schools, maintained secondary schools and technical colleges were implemented.

The Education Act of 1944 laid responsibility for the provision of primary and secondary schooling, and a range of other educational services, upon the councils of counties and county boroughs as LEAs. Second tier authorities were also permitted. By 1974 however, some 164 LEAs and 172 excepted districts and divisional executives in England and Wales had been reconstituted into 104 metropolitan, county and London authorities. Considerable variations in size and policy still continued. The population of Lancashire is some thirteen times greater than that of the Isle of Wight. Six different models of comprehensive reorganisation were outlined in Circular 10/65. Policy making at the local level is a complex process in which the personalities of the chairman of the education committee, a political appointment, and of the Chief Education Officer, may bulk large. In 1978 local education authorities employed some 1,385,000 persons, only 676,000 of whom worked in a teaching capacity.[21]

Though central government control of local authority expenditure appears to be on the increase, the public education service of this country remains immediately under local control. It is the principal item on local authority budgets. Indeed LEAs have direct responsibility for about 86 per cent of all public money spent on education. In the most recent development stemming from the later 1960s LEAs acquired further powers in higher education, when in accordance with the Labour government's 'binary system',[22] they were given charge of the new polytechnics.

Teachers

Whilst kings, clerics, ministers, politicians and administrators have exercised great influence on the control and organisation of English education, what of teachers, the key personnel in the educational process?

In the Middle Ages, although a variety of clerical and lay positions in society carried specific educational responsibilities, the independent, professional dimensions of teaching at both university and grammar school levels were clearly established. The degree of Master of Arts of a medieval university might theoretically give the right of teaching everywhere, indeed the newly-qualified MA, often to his regret, for financial rewards were slight, was required to lecture at the university for a period of up to two years.

Grammar schools, whether controlled and organised by cathedral or other churches for the supply of clerics, or by lay patrons or municipal bodies, required masters qualified and able to teach Latin grammar. Such men were often in short supply, as in 1439 when William Byngham deplored the fact that in the previous fifty years some seventy or more schools in that part of the country which lay to the south of Ripon and east of a line through Coventry and Hampton had been closed for lack of masters of grammar. Byngham accordingly successfully petitioned the King for permission to establish a new institution at Cambridge, God's House, later to be refounded in 1505 as Christ's College. The original foundation over which Byngham himself presided was for students who were required to graduate in grammar and accept appointments as schoolmasters, a master's degree in grammar having been introduced in the fourteenth century. Palmer and birch were bestowed upon its recipients as badges of office, and the new master was required to beat 'a shrewd boy ... openly in the Schools'[23] to show his proficiency in this essential schoolmasterly skill. A university degree remained the normal qualification for grammar school masters until the twentieth century. In the 1980s a university degree and licence to teach have for the first time in English history become universal requirements for virtually all new entrants to the school teaching profession.[24]

It has been suggested that the late sixteenth and early seventeenth centuries saw a period of significant development in the profession of schoolmastering. The careers and writings of such notable schoolmasters as Richard Mulcaster headmaster for twenty-five years of Merchant Taylors' and for eleven years of St Paul's, of John Brinsley master of the grammar school at Ashby de la Zouche, and Charles Hoole schoolmaster at Rotherham and in London, are adduced as evidence. Nevertheless, the low social status and poor financial rewards of teaching remained a common complaint. Many on graduating immediately secured licensing both for teaching and the curacy. Grammar school teaching was in many instances but a short term occupation. After a few years the ambitious young schoolmaster would progress to the greater security of a benefice with a substantial parsonage and further income from glebe and tithe. Poverty was a major problem, thus Mulcaster complained 'Why should not teachers be well provided for, to continue their whole life in the schools, as Divines, Lawyers, Physicians do in their several professions?'[25]

Though there were clear divisions between bishops and curates, barristers and solicitors, physicians, barber surgeons and apothecaries, teachers from the sixteenth to the nineteenth centuries presented a far greater heterogenity. Above the grammar school master and his usher were the teachers in universities, below him the teachers in petty, charity and other common schools. Amongst his rivals would be the teachers of private schools and academies, and a range of private tutors from those like Locke and Priestley[26] whose wideranging talents were at the service of the children and households of the greatest families in the land, to visiting masters with but one single social skill, music, dance or a modern language, to impart.

This bewildering variety of status and function made it more difficult for teachers, or any significant group of teachers, to become organised into a professional body, the standard means whereby lawyers, physicians and others came to control their particular areas of knowledge and expertise. Teaching, in the public view, was largely a part time or *faute de mieux* occupation, whether practised by clerics, their wives and daughters, small farmers, shopkeepers, cobblers, ex-soldiers, weavers, spinsters, widows and the like. Nevertheless teachers had considerable authority within their schools. The master of a grammar school was considered to have a freehold in his office, the owner and teacher of a private school had complete control, running a business like any other.

The advent of compulsory elementary and secondary schooling required the creation of a large full-time teaching force. In the nineteenth and twentieth centuries, however, teachers failed to produce a single professional governing body which might have organised and controlled, amongst other matters, standards of entry, qualification, practice, conduct and remuneration for the profession as a whole.

The National Union of Elementary Teachers (NUET later NUT) was founded in 1870, the Association of Headmistresses in 1874 and Assistant Mistresses ten years later. These latter, together with Associations of Headmasters (1890) and Assistant Masters (1891), formed the 'Joint Four' to represent the interests of headteachers and teachers in secondary grammar schools. The Association of University Teachers (AUT) was founded in 1919 initially to protect the superannuation rights of academic staff.

Some teachers attained considerable prominence. The headmaster of a major nineteenth-century public school enjoyed wealth, power and status not only in respect to his school, but also in the associated worlds of church and university, and in society at large. Though Eton was largely inbred, headmasters and even assistant masters of Harrow and Rugby provided a glut of archbishops of Canterbury, including Benson, Longley, Tait and Temple. The Headmasters' Conference (HMC) of the late nineteenth and early twentieth centuries was indeed a gathering of 'very superior men'.[27]

Teachers of children from the lower and middling classes, however, were held in low social esteem. Sunday schools, the first of the mass educational movements of the new society were staffed by part time teachers whose exact social status and role is a matter of some dispute.[28] Though monitorial schools of the early nineteenth century might be purpose built and even presided over by a 'trained' teacher, the whole system relied upon a process of mutual pupil instruction. In the 1840s unpaid monitors were replaced as the staple teaching force by paid apprentices — the pupil teachers. Training colleges were controlled by the religious organisations, whilst certification and inspection proceeded directly from the central government.

The nineteenth-century elementary teacher was the key figure in a complex process of control. His masters were the managers and the HMI. This visiting dignitary, to whose exalted ranks he dare not directly aspire, was, with the introduction in the 1860s of the Revised Code, both his annual inquisitor and virtual paymaster. It was the teacher's duty, for a mere pittance and the doubtful privilege of a lowly and isolated social position, to gentle the masses, to rescue the perishing, to bring order, propriety, deference and Christianity to fidgety, unwashed, uncouth children from hovel, tenement and slum. Some teachers were schooled to this task more rigorously than their pupils, in monastic training colleges where they were themselves taught to be humble, religious, respectable, dedicated and, according to much understanding of the time, entirely apolitical. The regimen was all-pervasive. Few facilities existed for relaxation, and in truth few were needed, for there was as scant opportunity in the training college timetable for recreation or association as there was for independence of thought. These traditions of training which combined great strengths as well as weaknesses persisted into the colleges of education of the twentieth century. Nevertheless even in 1898 more than half the female teachers and nearly 30 per cent of the male teachers in public elementary schools were untrained; both proportions significantly higher than in 1875.[29] Training for secondary teaching began in its modern form in the 1890s when secondary departments were set up in eight day training colleges.

In the twentieth century most teachers have become employees of local authorities, though salaries are determined at national level. No single professional body has as yet emerged. Nevertheless a decline in the birth rate, the acceptance of the married woman career teacher, and the development of secondary and higher education, has made possible the prospect of an all-graduate, trained teaching force. The independent tradition of training associated with Lancaster and Kay-Shuttleworth has come to an end. Of some 160 colleges of education in the 1960s the majority have been merged with other institutions or simply closed.

Since 1944 teachers in England and Wales have enjoyed considerable autonomy in such matters as curricula, syllabus, teaching and disciplinary methods. In the 1980s, however, teachers will probably be faced with demands for greater accountability. The very concept of professional freedom is under attack, not only from politicians and administrators, but also from parents and students. The 1977 Taylor report entitled *A New Partnership For Our Schools* recommended the equal representation on governing bodies of teachers, parents, LEAs and local community, with some provision for pupils as well. Such bodies, it was argued, should prescribe the aims and monitor the achievements of the school, on the grounds that education, even in schools, was too important to be left to teachers alone.

Examinations

In feudal society access to positions of authority was largely determined by factors of birth, patronage and gender. Their application can still be seen in such survivals from the medieval period as the monarchy and the House of Lords. Twentieth-century English society is bureaucratic, collectivist and professional. It has been described as 'capitalism tempered by competitive education'. It depends upon 'the organised application of trained intelligence'.[30] Examinations have been the key means both of establishing standards of trained intelligence and of conducting competitive education.

The vocational education of medieval England involved an element of practical examination. The young squire would need to acquit himself in the tournament or upon the battlefield. The skills of the young craftsman would be judged in the quality of his masterpiece. Just as the masters of the craft controlled the gild, so the masters or senior members controlled the university. Students proceeded by degrees: firstly as bachelors, then as masters, a qualification which accorded the right to teach.

The modern degree system dates from the middle of the eighteenth century. Reform began at Cambridge with the introduction of the Mathematical Tripos[31] with written as well as oral questions, and the publication of an honours list. Law and Classical Triposes were added in the early nineteenth century. Moral science, natural science and theology followed in the 1850s, history in the 1870s. Thus the ordinary or 'poll' degree man became the exception rather than the rule. Change at Oxford dates from the Examination Statute of 1800. By the middle of the century the Oxford University Commissioners claimed that 'the examinations have become the chief instruments, not only for testing the proficiency of the students, but also for stimulating and directing the studies of the place'.[32]

From 1862 examinations in elementary schools were organised under the Revised Code which established six standards of attainment. Other governmental intervention came through the Science and Art Department which provided grants and prizes to encourage the teaching of these subjects throughout the second half of the nineteenth century. In 1903, 75,956 papers were taken in science and 89,992 in art.

The Society of Arts had been founded in 1754, as an association for the promotion and encouragement of art, commerce, industry and invention. Premiums and prizes were awarded, and in the nineteenth century the society had connections with a variety of ventures including mechanics' institutes and the Great Exhibition. Its system of examinations began inauspiciously enough in 1854 with only one candidate. By 1913 there were some 30,000 candidates annually, and by 1953 over 150,000 candidates were taking RSA examinations. Competition from the examinations of the Science and Art Department and of the City and Guilds of London Institute in art, science and technical subjects propelled the RSA into the commercial field. Shorthand was added to its list of examination subjects in 1876, typewriting in 1891.

The City and Guilds of London Institute, formed in 1878 and incorporated in 1880, was financed by wealthy City livery companies. The Institute took over the technological examinations of the RSA and in 1908 had over 13,000 candidates. In 1949 there were 63,716 candidates and a range of 170 subjects. In 1975 some 433,000 students were following City and Guilds courses in over 300 subjects.

The College of Preceptors, founded by teachers in 1846 and granted a Royal Charter of Incorporation three years later, was another independent examining body. Some 17,000 school candidates were examined in 1893 but further development was hampered by the Board of Education's refusal to grant recognition to the examinations of the College on the same terms as those conducted by the universities.

In 1858 Local Examinations were introduced by Oxford, Cambridge and Durham universities. These were to be taken by pupils in middle-class schools. In 1865 girls were admitted to the Cambridge examinations, and a 'Higher Local' was instituted in 1869. 'Army Leaving Certificates', giving exemption from certain Army entrance examinations, were introduced by both Oxford and Cambridge Boards in 1905.

In 1868 the report of the Taunton Commissioners proposed a state-organised system of examinations for 'secondary' schools. As this was not implemented the universities, both old and new, came forward to supply the need. London University, which had been established in 1836 with Government financial assistance as an examining and degree awarding body, in particular became the centre of a world-wide examination system. In 1902 the University Senate approved the introduction of a School Leaving Certificate (Matriculation standard). Success in this examination qualified a candidate for university entrance. A Junior Certificate was added in the following year for those leaving at fifteen years of age.

In 1911 the Consultative Committee on Examinations in Secondary Schools recommended some rationalisation of the varying standards and practices of secondary school examinations. In 1917 a Secondary School Examinations Council was established, composed of representatives of the university examining bodies, teachers and local authorities, under a chairman appointed by the Board of Education.

Two levels of examination were consolidated. The first, the School Certificate Examination, was to test a good general education at the end of a five year grammar school course. The Higher School Certificate was to be taken after a further two years in the sixth form. In 1951 these examinations were replaced by the General Certificate of Education Examinations at Ordinary and Advanced levels. A competitive element was introduced with Scholarship level papers, primarily for the awarding of State Scholarships for university aspirants. GCE examinations, however, were still geared to secondary grammar schools, both in terms of subjects and of standards. In the 1950s the Associated Examining Board was established with a particular remit to supply papers in such novel subjects as electronics and food science. Secondary age pupils of lower ability, however, still relied upon the examinations of such bodies as the College of Preceptors, the London Chamber of Commerce and the Royal Society of Arts.

A new examination, the Certificate of Secondary Education (CSE), was designed to cater for the next 40 per cent of the ability range. GCE was considered suitable for the top 20 per cent. Introduced in the mid 1960s, CSE was organised on a regional basis with considerable teacher participation and control, and a variety of examining methods. A common examination at sixteen is now proposed.[33]

A complex structure of professional and vocational examinations has also developed in the twentieth century. Ordinary and Higher National Certificates for part time, Diplomas for full time students in technical subjects date from the 1920s. In 1975 there were some 36,000 HNC, 63,000 ONC, 20,000 HND and 25,000 OND students. Following the Haslegrave Report of 1969, however, the Technician Education Council (TEC) and Business Education Council (BEC) provided a new structure for validation of courses in the further education field. The Diploma of Technology (Dip Tech), an award of degree equivalence was born in the 1950s only to expire in the next decade. University degrees continued to enjoy a superior status, though from 1964 this monopoly was challenged with the establishment by royal charter of the Council for National Academic Awards (CNAA). The Council was empowered to grant degrees in a variety of subjects at bachelor, master and doctorate levels. In 1979–80 there were more than 1000 CNAA-validated courses, the great majority in the polytechnic sphere.

In the second half of the nineteenth century competitive education also developed rapidly. In 1854 the Northcote-Trevelyan Report recommended that recruitment to public service be conducted by competitive examination. This method was used for both civilian and military entrants to the Indian Service from 1854. In 1855 amidst the administrative fiasco of the Crimean War the Civil Service Commissioners were established as a potential examining agency. In 1859 the Commissioners assumed responsibility for the India Office examinations, and in 1870 for the entrance examinations to the military colleges at Sandhurst and Woolwich. In the same year an Order in Council made provision for the eventual extension of competitive entry to all branches of the Civil Service. Commission purchase in the army was abolished in 1871.

By the last decade of the nineteenth century payment by results was in decline, and this form of examination thus ceased to dominate the work of the elementary schools. A new breed of examinations were being developed, however, to assist in the task of selecting pupils for secondary schools. The scholarship system promoted considerable research into the best means of selection. In particular there was a concern to measure potential, to identify an intelligence quotient (IQ), rather than attainment which might be unduly influenced by school or home. By the later 1920s intelligence tests had become a salient feature in the selection procedures of many local authorities. The eleven plus examination, as it was generally known, remained a controversial issue throughout the 1960s and 70s.

Thus over the last two hundred years, in spite of many doubts and objections, public examinations have become a central feature both of the formal educational system and of English society. Examinations constituted in themselves a qualitatively new form of control and disciplinary power, a power which depended upon their being controlled by persons or bodies of high and independent status. In the nineteenth century this mantle fell particularly upon the universities of Cambridge, Oxford and London. Even in humble elementary schools annual examinations were conducted by

HMIs of considerable academic and social standing. For example in 1860, just prior to the introduction of payment by results, a third of the thirty-six Anglican inspectors had been fellows of Oxford or Cambridge colleges. Some indeed were of titled parentage, though inspectors were mainly recruited from the wealthy middle class.[34] Examinations have been seen as part of the nineteenth-century, 'middle-class' reform of education, and as a key instrument in the development of rational schooling. Their influence can be traced in knowledge and curricula, with an emphasis upon what can be measured and tested, in the aims, methods and organisation of teaching and learning, and even in the very rationale of some educational institutions. The crammers which prepared the young Winston Churchill and other aspiring entrants to Sandhurst in the nineteenth century have had their counterparts in the coaching establishments for the eleven plus, Common Entrance or GCE examinations in the twentieth. In a broader sense, in an age of meritocracy and division of labour, examinations have become an essential method of identification and selection. They have produced the age of the 'calculable' man and woman.

Conclusion

On occasions the history of education has been written simply in terms of the organisation over the last two hundred years of a formal schooling system under increasing central and local government control. One of the overall purposes of this book is to enlarge this particular perspective. Two particular conclusions can be drawn from the examples examined in this chapter. Firstly, governmental intervention in education has been a permanent feature of English history. Secondly, the organisation and control of education has been not only a matter of statutory, legal and administrative dimensions, but also of those less tangible influences which stem from professional, academic and other sources.

NOTES

1 **D. Cressy,** *Education in Tudor and Stuart England* (1975), p. 42.
2 **T.W. Laqueur,** *Religion and Respectability* (1976), p. 38.

3 **J. Murphy,** *Church, State and Schools in Britain, 1800–1970* (1971), p. 37.
4 **M. Cruickshank,** *Church and State in English Education 1870 to the Present Day* (1963), p. 18.
5 **The Education Act of 1870** provided for the establishment of local School Boards. The voluntary schools were 'overmatched' (a boxing term) by the heavyweight board schools which would draw upon rates as well as government grants and parental contributions. School Boards were abolished in 1902.
6 **Murphy** (1971), p. 125.
7 **Sylvester** (1970), p. 49.
8 **John Colet** (*c*. 1467–1519), dean of St Paul's and founder of St Paul's School; **William Lily** (c. 1468–1522), its first high master.
9 **William Laud** (1573–1645), impeached by the House of Commons and beheaded.
10 **John Pym** (1584–1643), who promoted Laud's impeachment; **John Hampden** (1594–1643), who in 1636 led the opposition to ship money; **Oliver Cromwell** (1599–1658) who promoted the trial and execution of Charles I in 1649 and in 1653 became Protector of the Commonwealth.
11 **The Home Secretary, Lord John Russell's** scheme is printed in J.S. Maclure, *Educational Documents England and Wales 1816 to the present day* (1979), pp. 42–5.
12 **James Kay-Shuttleworth** (1804–77), doctor, assistant poor law commissioner and secretary to the Committee of Privy Council on Education 1839–49.
13 **J.S. Hurt,** *Education in Evolution* (1971), p. 164.
14 **The Lord President of the Council** was invariably a member of the House of Lords. Robert Lowe (1811–92), author of the Revised Code and W.E. Forster (1818–86), architect of the Education Act of 1870 were the two most famous Vice Presidents.
15 **Specific** subjects enabled individual pupils to earn extra grants for their schools, **Class** subjects were examined on the proficiency of the whole class.
16 **Maclure** (1979), p. 223.
17 These changes are well summarised in E.J.R. Eaglesham, *The Foundations of 20th Century Education in England* (1967).
18 **Non-county boroughs** with more than 10,000 population and urban districts with more than 20,000 (the Part III authorities) were given control over elementary education only. In 1944 Part III authorities were abolished although 35 achieved a new subordinate status as 'excepted' districts.
19 **M. Seaborne,** *Recent Education from Local Sources* (1967); pp. 38–9.
20 **J.S. Maclure,** *One Hundred Years of London Education 1870–1970* (1970), p. 116.

21 Figures quoted in E. Midwinter, *Schools in Society* (1980), p. 98.
22 **The binary system,** implemented from the later 1960s, provided an alternative form of higher education under local government control.
23 **Sylvester** (1970), p. 71. The palmer was for use on the pupil's hands.
24 This was made possible by a drastic reduction of the numbers of teachers in training, and by the replacement of the Teachers Certificate by the Bachelor of Education (B Ed) degree. It is still possible, however, to teach Maths and Science without training.
25 Quoted in E.B. Castle, *The Teacher* (1970), p. 92.
26 **Joseph Priestley** (1733–1804), chemist and Presbyterian minister.
27 **A.C. Percival,** *Very Superior Men: Some early Public School Headmasters and their Achievements* (1973).
28 *See* for example Laqueur (1976) and M. Dick, 'The myth of the working-class Sunday school', *History of Education* (1980), 9 (1).
29 **A.C.O. Ellis,** 'The Training and Supply of Teachers in the Victorian Period', *History of Education Society Bulletin* (1979), 24, p. 22.
30 **H. Perkin,** *Key Profession* (1969) p. 1.
31 **Tripos,** derived from the earlier custom of sitting on a three legged stool when debating in the Philosophy School.
32 Quoted in R.J. Montgomery, *Examinations* (1965), p. 14 from which many of the following figures are taken.
33 **In October 1980** the DES issued a consultative paper *Examinations 16–18* which confirmed that the dual system of GCE O-level and CSE would be replaced by 'a single system of clearly defined grades, with national criteria for syllabuses and assessment procedures'.
34 **Hurt** (1971), p. 176.

4　Primary Education

Medieval Origins

Parents and priests

In medieval society fundamental education for all was primarily religious, moral, social and vocational. It was a father's duty to instruct his sons in the means of earning their daily bread, and a mother's to prepare her daughters for the domestic role. Education thus took place in a family context; in field and workshop, in home and market place. Basic religious instruction for all, both old and young, together with some provisions for rudimentary male literacy were also enjoined. Thus from the tenth century the canons of King Edgar required 'that every Christian man zealously accustom his children to Christianity and teach them the Pater Noster and Creed'.[1] Particular responsibility for the education of young males lay with the parish priest. Councils from the tenth and twelfth centuries ordained 'That priests shall keep schools in the villages and teach little boys *gratis*'.[2]

It was the parish priest's duty to instruct all his flock in religious matters. In 1281, for example, the constitution *Ignorantia sacerdotum*, reissued until the sixteenth century, prescribed a basic summary of Christian doctrine and morality which all should learn — the ten commandments, the seven sacraments, and so on. Such instruction might proceed principally from the pulpit, but other means tantamount to schooling might also be employed. Parish clerks, moreover, were required to keep song schools to train boys as choristers, a widely-followed practice as indicated in the example of Lincoln where in 1305 the cathedral songmaster sought to reassert his right to license such schools.[3] Reading and song were a recognised preliminary stage prior to the learning of Latin grammar, as in the case of the seven year old 'litel clergeon' in Chaucer's *Prioress's Tale*. They were frequently studied in the same school, though at Winchester from the beginning of the fifteenth century, and at Eton from 1447, scholars were required to have completed their studies in reading, song and basic grammar prior to entry. The first such example from the six counties of the West of England, however, dates only from 1520 when the statutes of Bruton school forbade the master to teach the alphabet, reading and song, in order that he might concentrate upon grammar teaching.[4]

The principal purpose of the song schools of the later middle ages whether connected with cathedral, parish church or chantry college, was to instruct boys to sing plainsong, and in some instances the more elaborate choral polyphonic settings. Such skills would also be essential for those who later as clergy, in whatever capacity, would be required daily to perform the divine office. By 1547, however, chantry priests were ordered by royal injunction to 'exercise themselves in teaching youths to read and write'.[5] This may be seen not merely as a consequence of the Reformation, but also as a logical extension of the developing facilities for elementary schooling of the previous one hundred and fifty years. Evidence for this is provided by an apparently rapid growth in the numbers of parish, song, reading and writing schools in the diocese of York in the fifteenth century.[6] The use from the fourteenth century of written English has been adduced as one reason for such growth.

Three examples may be given of schools founded in the 1480s. At Newland in Gloucestershire Robert Gryndour founded a school where quarterly fees were 8d for those learning grammar, and 4d for those merely learning to read.[7] Jesus College, established by the Archbishop of York at Rotherham in 1483, provided three free schools — of grammar, song and writing. The teacher in this third school was to be 'learned and skilled in the art of writing and accounts', in order that his pupils might become 'better fitted for the mechanical arts and other concerns of this world'.[8] In 1489 William Chamber made a bequest for a chantry chaplain to celebrate daily masses for the souls of himself and his wife Elizabeth in the parish church of Aldwincle, Northamptonshire. The chaplain was also required, without fee, to 'teach and instruct in spelling and reading, six of the poorest boys of the town'.[9]

The alphabet

It is impossible from the fragmentary evidence which remains to determine the extent and effectiveness of elementary education and schooling in the medieval period. We are particularly ignorant of the processes whereby writing was taught prior to the sixteenth century. Nevertheless some basic features do emerge. Elementary schooling generally began with the alphabet. By the fourteenth century this had been standardised as follows.[10]

+A.a.b.c.d.e.f.g.h.i.k.
l.m.n.o.p.q.r.ꝛ.ſ.s.t.
v.u.x.y.z.&.ꝯ.∴.est amen.

Thus it began with a reminder to the child to make the sign of the cross, and then proceeded with capital 'A', followed by lower case letters with alternative forms for 'r', 's' and 'u'. Abbreviations for *et* and *con* were followed by the three dots or tittles, and concluded with the *est amen*.The alphabet survived in this form with only minor modifications until the eighteenth century.

The alphabet would be presented to children in different ways. It might be written in large letters upon the whitewashed wall of the church vestry, porch or other building which served as a schoolroom. Alternatively letters might be written on parchment and fixed to a wooden board or tablet, like the horn books of the sixteenth century in which the letters were covered by a layer of translucent horn for their protection. Or again children might learn their letters from the primer, a small book which, beginning with the alphabet, continued to the Lord's Prayer, creed, ten commandments and other fundamentals of worship. From the thirteenth century, if not before, such primers were produced both in Latin and in English. Successful scholars would proceed from the primer to the service books, for example the psalter and the mattins book. This led naturally into the dimension of song which assisted in the correct pronounciation of Latin words even by those who did not understand their meanings.

Schoolboys

'Song' schools together with 'reading' schools were the elementary schools of the medieval period, and some of their features have continued in the training received by church choirboys from that day to this. The following extract from the rules governing the choir school attached to Westminster Abbey in the thirteenth century appears to indicate that in some respects boys themselves have changed little in seven hundred years.

> Then, after they have made up the beds properly, let them leave their room together quietly, without clattering and approach the church modestly with washed hands, not running or skipping, or even chattering, or having a row with any person or animal; not carrying bow or staff, or stone in the hand ... Whether they are standing or sitting in the choir, let them not have their eyes turned aside to the people, but rather toward the altar; not grinning, or chattering, or laughing aloud; not making fun of another if he does not read or sing psalms well; not hitting one another secretly or openly, or answering rudely if they happen to be asked a question by their elders ...
>
> Again, whoever at bedtime has torn to pieces the bed of his companions or hidden the bedclothes, or thrown shoes or pillows from corner to corner, or roused anger, or thrown the school into disorder, shall be severely punished in the morning.[11]

Sixteenth to Eighteenth Centuries

Social and economic change

The inhabitants of sixteenth-century England and Wales experienced profound economic, social, political and religious changes. Runaway inflation, fed by the influx of precious metals from the New World, and by successive debasements of the coinage, reached a peak in the 1540s but continued largely unchecked for another hundred years. Those on fixed incomes, including no doubt many teachers and parents, suffered greatly. Unemployment presented an even more pressing problem. During the sixteenth century the population increased by about a third, to some four million in 1600. Concern to counter the resultant mobility, poverty and vagrancy, particularly as represented by the spectre of the 'sturdy beggar', was reflected both in private charity and in legislation. In parish schools, workhouses and other contexts, great stress was placed upon preparing poor and pauperised children for employment.

In 1536 Royal injunctions declared the need for universal religious and occupational training.

> The parsons, vicars and other curates aforesaid shall diligently admonish the fathers and mothers, masters and governors of youth,

being within their cure, to teach or cause to be taught their children and servants, even from their infancy, their *pater noster*, the articles of our faith, and the ten commandments, in their mother tongue ... that the said fathers and mothers, masters and governors do bestow their children and servants, even from their childhood, either to learning or to some other honest exercise, occupation or husbandry ... that the said youth be in no manner wise kept or brought up in idleness, lest at any time afterwards they be driven for lack of some mystery or occupation to live by, to fall to begging, stealing or some other unthriftiness.[12]

In 1563, by the Statute of Artificers, though parental property qualifications were still demanded for entry to skilled trades, the seven year apprenticeship system was extended virtually to all urban crafts. During Elizabeth's reign Justices of the Peace and town officers were empowered to establish workhouse schools and to bind the children of vagrants, paupers, and even of those who might become a charge upon the parish, in the service of any householder. After 1570 at Norwich, however, some 900 children of the poor whose parents could not afford to pay for their schooling were organised in an employment training scheme for which they received 6d a week.[13] Women were appointed in each ward of the city to instruct the children in spinning and other skills.

The Reformation

Elementary education in religious matters, reading and writing took place in a variety of private, petty and parish schools. These might be kept by men and women primarily engaged in other occupations — shopkeepers, spinsters, weavers, cobblers — by curates and parish clerks, or even by the usher or master of the local grammar school. Some were endowed and free, but many parents paid fees, in addition to foregoing the value of their children's labour. The alphabet and the fundamentals of the Christian faith as set forth in Bible and prayer book were the subjects of study, and English the usual language of instruction. Horn book and primer were basic aids to learning, and in 1545 an authorised primer was issued by royal injunction. Boys and girls, particularly in urban areas, might proceed from the petties to other 'English' schools for further instruction in reading, writing, arithmetic and accounts.

It is impossible to determine the precise effect of the Protestant reformation upon the provision of elementary education. In the 1530s the dissolution of the monasteries no doubt led to the loss of some song schools. Similarly in Edward VI's reign the suppression of the chantries, in spite of the provisions of the Act of 1547 which required the continuation of educational facilities connected with these institutions, probably produced a net reduction in schooling at the elementary level. On the other hand the undoubted growth of grammar schools in the years 1560–1640, a growth not unconnected with religious and other consequent social and economic changes, might well have stimulated rather than hindered the provision of general primary schooling and of itinerant writing masters.

Civil War

The years 1640–60 were years of upheaval, and of radical political and religious change. Some educational theorists of the period, notably Comenius, Hartlib, Dury, Petty and their circle, proposed radical educational changes as well. These included elementary schooling for all, boys and girls alike. Curricula were to be made useful and interesting, and learning to become a pleasure rather than a pain. Schoolteaching, including that of young children, was to be recognised as a high calling.

In fact, however, the most celebrated educational work of the period, Milton's *Of Education* (1644),[14] was amongst the more conservative, and concerned with the secondary and higher stages. In spite of the climate of ideas and the resources available from sequestered church property, parliamentary educational legislation in this period promised little and achieved less. Hartlib and his group acknowledged the necessity of state intervention to secure worthwhile universal schooling, but the new religious orthodoxy of the Commonwealth took precedence over, or perhaps constituted the main aim of, educational reform. In consequence their most likely educational heirs, the protestant dissenters, became in their turn the most extreme of educational independents. For some two hundred years after 1660 dissenting congregations opposed state intervention in elementary education in fear that the influence of the Anglican church would thereby be increased.

In the later seventeenth and eighteenth centuries many Englishmen and women saw the need for a period of stability, and in particular for an end to civil and religious strife. They deplored the years of the civil war and of the interregnum, events which were attributed in part to the overprovision of grammar school and university places. Charitable provision for education was thus directed to the elementary level.

Charity schooling

In the medieval period poverty was a virtue to be cultivated, and charity principally of benefit to the giver. From the later sixteenth century, however, poverty was to be seen rather as a danger and a sin, the result of idleness and ignorance — a condition to be combatted and controlled. The charity of the late seventeenth century took place at a time of the visibly growing poverty of the many as against the visibly increasing wealth of the few. Charity schooling was to benefit both giver and recipient. Children of the poorer classes would be kept off the streets and farms, and the property of others protected thereby. They would be trained as good Christians, loyal citizens, and industrious workpeople. The pupils' uniforms were an advertisement in this world to the piety and good works of their benefactors, whilst their childish prayers of intercession would help to secure their own salvation and that of the founders and subscribers in the next.

Charity education for the poor was in schools which evolved from traditional parish patterns. Particular emphasis was placed upon the learning of the catechism as a bulwark against Roman Catholic doctrines, and from 1699 the Society for Promoting Christian Knowledge began to encourage the foundation of catechitical schools, both in London and Westminster, and subsequently throughout the country as a whole. Some charity schools were endowed with land or other means of regular income, others were supported by subscriptions, appeals and collections, particularly following upon an annual charity sermon. In some there was sufficient money to pay the teacher and to provide the children with uniforms, boarding and entry into apprenticeship. The charity children of London became a national institution and were paraded on state occasions. Thus in 1713 on a day of thanksgiving for the Treaty of Utrecht some 3,925 charity children, boys and girls new clothed, with masters and mistresses were seated on an eight tiered gallery in the Strand in full view of both Houses of Parliament in their procession to St Paul's. In the following year on the occasion of George I's entry to the City an even larger number of charity children were placed upon a machine 600 feet long and with six tiers of seats, on the north side of St Paul's. As the king passed by, and much to his delight, the children sang the twenty-first psalm.

The exact role of the SPCK in the provision of charity schooling has been a matter of some dispute.[15] By 1730, however, the initial impetus had diminished. Critics of the charity schools included

Bernard Mandeville who questioned the value of teaching reading, writing and arithmetic to the children of the labouring poor. In an essay of 1724 he argued that the charity schools of the eighteenth century were simply repeating the errors of the excessive school provision of the sixteenth and seventeenth centuries, though at a lower social level: 'Going to school in comparison to working, is idleness, and the longer boys continue in this easy sort of life, the more unfit they will be when grown up for downright labour, both as to strength and inclination'.[16]

In reply, however, it was argued that charity schools provided a Christian and a useful education, and inculcated habits of piety, virtue and deference. Though the catechism might be learned by heart, reading was necessary for a fuller understanding of the Bible and prayer book. Writing and arithmetic were taught more frequently to boys, and specifically for the purpose of fitting them for apprenticeship or other employment, whilst girls received instruction in household matters.

The implementation of this viewpoint that elementary schooling of the children of the lower orders, both boys and girls, was a legitimate and necessary stage *prior* to their employment, was probably the most significant development in the history of English education. Mandeville was expressing an age-old economic and social principle that the children of the poor must be put to work at the earliest possible age, though in deference to Christian beliefs for six rather than seven days per week. As an alternative to the charity school solution John Locke in a report of 1697 to the Board of Trade suggested the establishment of working schools in every parish. These would be attached to workhouses and cater for all unemployed children between the ages of three and fourteen. Training and work would be provided on weekdays with compulsory attendance at church on Sundays for religious and moral instruction.

Though Daniel Defoe,[17] in his tract *Giving Alms no Charity* (1704) sought to eliminate both workhouses and workhouse schools, workhouse provision increased during the eighteenth century, particularly after the general act of 1723. Workhouse and working schools on the Lockean model followed in their wake. A spinning school at Findon in Northamptonshire where girls were taught and wholly maintained from the proceeds of their own labour became the model working school of the period.[18] Some charity schools also came to be organised as schools of industry.

Such schools, however, rarely prospered. Overseers of the poor often sought rather to 'apprentice' their charges as soon and as far away as possible. Pitt's poor law scheme of 1795 which envisaged parish schools of industry with compulsory attendance of children whose parents were on the rates was never implemented.

Sunday schools

The Sunday school movement which grew rapidly from the 1780s was a reformulation, at a time of rapid population growth and industrial and urban development, of traditional means of educational supply. Once more education in religious and moral matters together with some appropriate literary instruction was provided on Sundays by part-time teachers in part-time premises for children and some adults who had few other opportunities of formal schooling. In 1839 a general survey of handloom weavers showed that five times as many of their children attended Sunday school as weekday school. Of nearly 3,000 such children in twenty parishes in Gloucestershire less than 10 per cent were in day schools but two thirds attended Sunday schools.[19]

It is difficult to determine the numbers of schools and scholars in the early period, but by 1831 there were over one million enrolled in Sunday schools in England, and more than two million in 1851. These constituted 8.4 per cent and 12.5 per cent respectively of the total population, and 49.6 per cent and 75.4 per cent respectively of working class children aged five to fifteen years. Sunday schools were at their most popular during the early years of compulsory daily elementary schooling. In 1881 19 per cent of the total population of England, Scotland and Wales were enrolled in them. Thereafter the proportion declined, to stand at 11 per cent in 1931 and 5 per cent in 1961.[20]

Sunday schools stand at the crossroads of modern English and Welsh educational history. They exhibited many of the features of traditional elementary education. Robert Raikes'[21] determination to reform society through the Sunday school 'by establishing notions of duty and discipline at an early stage',[22] is typical of eighteenth century religious reformism. The widespread evangelical movement of the time even permitted the formation of interdenominational or nondenominational bodies, the Sunday School Society of 1785, the Sunday School Union of 1803, and, in a different context the British and Foreign School Society of 1814. Many Sunday schools were based upon church or chapel, organised by the clergy, their wives and daughters, and continued to impart religious and moral instruction above all other.

Though the ultimate purposes of duty and discipline were seen by Raikes and his contemporaries in a variety of ways, including salvation, preservation of property and the peace of the sabbath, particular emphasis has been placed by some historians on the concern to produce an amenable workforce. Sunday schools, it has been argued, were an important means whereby members of the upper and middle classes sought to suppress the pre-industrial behaviour patterns of the labouring classes and replace them with those habits of punctuality, regular attendance, honesty, deference and sobriety so essential to factory employment. Such virtues, however, were neither exclusively industrial, nor middle-class. T.W. Laqueur has argued that Sunday schools with their quarter of a million teachers by 1851 drawn largely from the ranks of former scholars, their secular instruction, outings, anniversaries and prizes, should be seen as a new expression of popular culture rather than simply as an alien imposition.[23] One particular aspect of this popular culture was to be found in Wales. In the late seventeenth and early eighteenth centuries the charity schools of the Welsh Trust and the SPCK had used English as the medium of instruction. In sharp contrast both Griffith Jones, founder of the circulating schools which flourished between 1737 and 1779, and Thomas Charles, pioneer of the principality's Sunday schools, emphasized the importance of teaching in Welsh.

Nineteenth and Twentieth Centuries

Monitorial schools

From the later eighteenth-century population increase, urbanisation and industrialisation transformed some aspects of economic and social life in a manner which can legitimately be described as revolutionary. In some parts of the country within a generation, a decade, even within a year, the traditional means of supplying such necessities of life as water, food, housing, sanitation, employment, poor relief, religion and education became inadequate. Instant solutions were sought to such instant problems. One instant solution applied to elementary education in the first thirty years of the nineteenth century, and on occasion to secondary education too, was the monitorial or mutual system of schooling.

Its independent inventors, the Quaker Joseph Lancaster, and the

Anglican clergyman Andrew Bell, were hailed as amongst the supreme benefactors of the human race. Their invention was favourably compared with other great discoveries of the age including the steam engine and vaccination. The monitorial system as set out in Bell's *An Experiment in Education made at the Male Asylum at Egremont, near Madras* (1797), or as practised at Lancaster's school in Borough Road, Southwark from 1798 and subsequently described in his *Improvements in Education, as it respects the Industrious Classes of the Community* (1803), promised a cheap, efficient and disciplined means of mass instruction. Large, not to say extravagant claims were made on its behalf. This new 'intellectual and moral engine', Bell maintained in *An Experiment in Education,* would produce better Christians, better scholars, better men and women, and better workers. Children would be taught 'to act their part and perform their duty in future life with punctuality, diligence, impartiality and justice', and 'to take an early and well-directed interest in the welfare of one another'. Whilst Lancaster claimed that one master could manage a school containing a thousand pupils, Bell contended that a master could supervise ten such contiguous schools.

The system required, therefore, but a single school room and one teacher, assisted by monitors or tutors with a variety of duties, instructional and disciplinary, chosen from amongst the older and abler pupils. Lancaster spelled out the teaching methods in minute detail. Drill, repetition and practice were central to his system of learning, but the monitor's responsibility was not simply to put his 'class' of children through their paces but also to create a system of mutual instruction. Co-operation and competition went hand in hand. An elaborate system of rewards was devised by Lancaster — merit badges, and prizes in cash or kind, tops, balls, kites, even silver pens and watches — according to the value of merit tickets collected.

Lancaster believed that most classroom misbehaviour was the result of exuberance rather than malevolence. His range of punishments was designed to isolate offenders and to expose them to the ridicule of their classmates. Public washing of those who came to school dirty, attachment of shackles to ankles or wrists, a log fixed around the neck, suspension from the ceiling in sack or basket — were designed for this purpose. Alternatively miscreants were detained after school hours. The continuous attendance of the teacher was to be dispensed with by the expedient of tying the children securely to their desks.

The monitorial system, like many other educational innovations before and since, was in vogue for some thirty years. There were obvious deficiencies. Mutual instruction of children was a common enough occurrence in the home, but many parents and children doubtless expected instruction within school to be directly imparted by an adult. Nevertheless it had the most important consequences for the history of nineteenth-century elementary schooling.

The two societies formed to carry on the work of Bell and Lancaster provided a network of 'National' and 'British' schools which covered the country. The National Society for Promoting the Education of the Poor in the Principles of the Established Church was set up in 1811. Presided over by the Archbishop of Canterbury, with York, London and the other bishops as vice-presidents, and with the diocesan organisation, personnel and resources of the State Church at its command, the National Society soon became the most powerful educational agency in the kingdom. In consequence the British and Foreign School Society, created in 1814 to succeed the Royal Lancasterian Society of 1808, numerically speaking was always a second best. It, however, adopted a more international role, and particularly in the early years commanded support from a broad political and denominational spectrum. Denominational rivalry in educational provision thus was redefined in the early nineteenth century. For example Sarah Trimmer in her *Comparative View of the New Plan of Education promulgated by Mr Joseph Lancaster* (1805), asserted that Lancaster had simply stolen Bell's ideas. Throughout the nineteenth century many Anglicans believed that a parish without a National school was a parish 'abandoned to the enemy'.

In 1833 when Parliament voted that 'a sum not exceeding Twenty thousand pounds be granted to His Majesty, to be issued in aid of Private Subscriptions for the Erection of School Houses, for the Education of the Children of the Poorer Classes in Great Britain', such money was given exclusively to the schools of the two societies. In the first five years of this grant system the National Society received seventy per cent of the money. Assistance was given to 714 of its schools as opposed to 187 British schools. Government grants, given at first for school building, were later extended to the provision of teachers and of teacher training. The monitorial system necessitated the training of teachers in a particular theory and method of instruction. Such training might be very short, a matter of days or weeks, but both Lancaster and Bell envisaged this as an essential part of the function of their respective establishments at Borough Road and Baldwins Gardens. Borough Road College, which now forms part of the West London Institute of Higher Education, is regarded as the most senior of modern English teacher training institutions. As with the schools, however, the majority of such nineteenth-century colleges, like St Mark's and Whitelands, were associated with the National Society and the Anglican Church.

Critics of the monitorial system included Robert Owen, who in 1816 gave evidence to Brougham's Select Committee on the Education of the Lower Orders. As an alternative Owen described his system at New Lanark where infant, day, evening and Sunday schooling was provided for children of the factory workers. Owen declared that one superior master or 'rector', and ten assistant teachers male and female, were necessary for the schooling of these 700 pupils. Under this scheme children were educated at an average cost of £1 per head per annum, an expense which Owen justified as the best means of 'forming the character and directing the labour of the lower classes'.[24] Other promoters of the schooling of infants were Samuel Wilderspin, missionary extraordinary of the London Infant School Society founded in 1824, and Charles Mayo whose Home and Colonial Infant School Society founded in 1836 opened a training college at Holborn in the same year.

Universal schooling

Legislative proposals for the establishment of elementary schooling in this period drew upon a variety of sources. Samuel Whitbread's bill of 1807 which would have entitled the children of poor parents to two years' free schooling, originated from a scheme for Poor Law reform. Like Brougham's parochial schools bill of 1820 it also owed much to the example of Scotland. Roebuck's unsuccessful scheme of 1833 drew upon the experience of public schooling in France, Prussia and certain states of the USA.[25] The Poor Law Amendment Act of 1834 envisaged the compulsory education of pauper children, but the general principle of 'less eligibility'[26] ensured the low status of workhouse schools. The educational clauses of the Factory Acts of 1802, 1819 and 1833, this last the first to be enforced by inspectors, continued the tradition of regulation of apprenticeship in industrial rather than rural occupations. In 1846 the principle of apprenticeship was finally applied to the craft of elementary school teaching. Dr James Kay-Shuttleworth, secretary to the Committee of Privy Council on Education established in

1839 was amongst the most ardent supporters of the scheme. Henceforth government financial aid to elementary schooling became more concerned with the provision of teachers than of school buildings. At the same time a new role was provided for the inspectors, the first of whom, John Allen and Seymour Tremenheere, had been appointed in 1840 to supervise the grants to National and British schools respectively.

By the middle of the nineteenth century day schooling had become an accepted means of providing education for virtually all the children in England. The Royal Commission under the chairmanship of the Duke of Newcastle which inquired into the state of popular education in the years 1858–61,[27] further implied that all children should, as a result of this schooling, acquire 'the power of reading, writing and cyphering in an intelligent manner'. Irregular attendance and inefficient teaching, it was concluded, were the principal obstacles to the attainment of this goal. The Commissioners acknowledged, however, that in certain families where a child's labour was necessary to keep the parents off the poor rates or to relieve severe poverty, 'it is better that it should go to work at the earliest age at which it can bear the physical exertion than that it should remain at school'.

The Commissioners reported on the steady extension of day school provision which had taken place since the beginning of the nineteenth century. In 1803 the numbers of day scholars in England and Wales in relation to the total population had been calculated at 1 in 17.5. In 1818 the figure was 1 in 17.25, in 1833 1 in 11.25, in 1851 1 in 8.36, and in 1858 1 in 7.7. This figure, though inferior to that of 1 in 6.27 in Prussia where schooling was compulsory, compared favourably with those of Holland, 1 in 8.11, and France, 1 in 9.0. The Commissioners calculated that only 120,305 children in England and Wales were without any form of school instruction. Of some 2,213,694 children of the poorer classes (321,768 children of the upper ranks of society having been excluded from the inquiry), 573,536 were on the books of private schools, and an impressive 1,549,312 on the books of the public elementary schools of the religious societies. Government grants were given in aid of 6,897 of these schools containing 917,255 pupils.

In the eighteenth and nineteenth centuries workhouse schools catered for children whose parents had failed them in an economic and social sense. Similarly many charity schools of the eighteenth century provided an intensive and all-embracing education for outcast, orphaned or deprived children whose parents were deemed to have yielded up their natural rights and authority to the school. In contrast the mass schooling of the nineteenth century, particularly in the period prior to 1870, was aimed principally at helping the independent and deserving poor to educate their children in an independent or semi-independent manner. National and British schools came to be regarded as the norm; ragged, industrial and other schools for the delinquent and dangerous classes as the exceptions. Government financial aid was not given to the poorest and most needy schools and teachers, but rather to those which promised to become or were already successful. Parents were expected to contribute directly to the cost of schooling their children, and in 1870 elementary schools were defined as those whose fees did not exceed 9d per scholar per week. In the monitorial schools at Leeds, for example, parents paid an average 1d per week per child from 1815 and 2d per week after 1840.[28]

Such parental independence, however, ensured the continuation of practices which were to be regretted both by the Newcastle Commissioners and by the growing vested interests involved in public elementary schooling. Thus in 1858 working-class parents chose to send over half a million children to private schools. These schools, the Commissioners believed to be 'for the most part, inferior as schools for the poor, and ill-calculated to give to the children an education which shall be serviceable to them in after-life'. Moreover, more than half the 1½ million children whose names were on the books of the public elementary schools belonging to the religious societies attended for less than 100 days per year.

Thus although by 1858 day schooling had become a normal means of supplying elementary education for children, a common curriculum with generally-accepted standards of attainment, and regular attendance had not. For example the Educational Census of 1851 revealed that while 98 per cent of the elementary schools in England and Wales taught reading, only 68 per cent taught writing and 61 per cent arithmetic. Industrial occupations were taught by a mere 2 per cent. The Revised Code of 1862 with its formula of payments in part upon the results achieved in the 3 Rs had a profound effect upon the curricula of inspected elementary schools, not least in Wales where no grants were given for proficiency in the vernacular. The Elementary Education Act of 1870 which permitted by-laws for compulsory attendance from the age of five was designed to ensure that there would be sufficient elementary school places of reasonable quality for all the nation's children. By 1880 it was possible to require compulsory school attendance at least until the age of ten, to be raised to eleven in 1893 and twelve in 1899. In 1891 all parents were given the right of free elementary schooling for their children.

The last three decades of the nineteenth century were controversial years in which large urban school boards were to the fore in redefining elementary education in terms of universal schooling. By the end of 1871, 117 school boards had instituted by-laws requiring some degree of compulsory attendance. By 1900 nearly half the children who attended public elementary schools were in board schools. In large urban areas the proportion was often much higher. In 1903 in London, 549,677 pupils were in board schools and only 213,297 in the voluntary schools.[29]

Public resistance to the ideal of compulsory universal schooling was based on grounds of genuine economic and social concern. The rash of new schools constructed after 1870, often in densely populated areas, caused a loss of housing and other amenities which may be likened to that caused by the building of urban motorways in the twentieth century. Since school boards were *ad hoc* bodies, concerned only with education, their members could raise the education rate without any need to consider the financial requirements of other local services. Parents, children, employers, and many magistrates, even Sir James Fitzjames Stephen of the Queen's Bench Division in the famous case of the *London School Board v Duggan 1884*, pointed out the irrelevance of the compulsory schooling of older children to families on the brink of starvation, or otherwise engaged in the struggle for sheer survival. To keep a child who had the opportunity of secure and profitable employment or some essential family duty, at school until the age of 13 or 14 simply because he or she was unable adequately to perform a series of arbitrary tests in the 3 Rs seemed nonsensical to a wide range of opinion in all classes of society. In 1872 the percentage attendance of pupils whose names were on the rolls of London elementary schools was 76.7. Twenty years later it stood at only 77.7.[30] In some schools the attendance was much lower, and continued to be so until the end of the nineteenth century.

Employment at home or elsewhere was not the only reason for non-attendance. The quality of instruction, even in grant-aided elementary schools, left much to be desired, and probably deteriorated in the period 1870–80. School boards had no powers to establish teacher training institutions, though some pupil-teacher centres were set up. In 1880 as in 1870 there were more than twice as many pupil teachers as college-trained certificated teachers employed in grant-aided elementary schools. Many parents and children refused to accept the authority of pupil teachers and demanded 'proper teachers' instead.

The limited nature of this compulsory education was another source of controversy. In previous centuries schooling of the children of the poorest classes had often included provision for their immediate physical well-being in terms of food and clothing, and for their subsequent employment. It was recognised that if parents were unable to provide for the moral and mental well-being of their offspring there was little logic in presuming them able to care for their health and welfare. In the later nineteenth century, however, when large numbers of the poorest children were being forced regularly to attend schools, many came hungry and remained so throughout the day. Some were in rags, or absent simply because they lacked the boots and outer clothing in which to make journeys to and from school. But the state which now required children to learn their letters and deprived them of the right to earn their own livelihood, refused to accept this further responsibility. In 1884 the inspector J.G. Fitch warned that 'a school is established for the purposes of instruction, and not for the purpose of dispensing new milk'. Fitch indeed condemned the charitable groups who provided free meals (though in truth many of them were highly unpalatable) on the grounds of the 'demoralising effect produced on many parents, who, not being paupers, are yet willing to claim free dinners for their little ones, and so to have more to spend on intemperance'.[31]

By 1905, however, attendance in London elementary schools had reached eighty-eight per cent of those on the roll,[32] a figure broadly comparable with that of London primary schools since the Second World War. Those in charge of the system, school board members, inspectors and visitors, teachers, and other observers, were wont to attribute this improved attendance to a general acceptance of the manifest benefits of education. On the other hand it seems possible that whilst the children of the 'respectable' working classes regularly went more or less willingly to school, other pupils complied rather through increasing force of habit than anything else. In 1895 only fourteen per cent of children in inspected elementary schools were aged twelve or over. Even this figure included a high proportion of reluctant attenders who through mental or physical handicap were unable to reach the necessary standard to obtain their release.

The original subjects and standards of the Revised Code of 1862 formed the basis of much elementary schooling in the later nineteenth century.[33]

	Standard I	Standard II	Standard III
Reading	Narrative in monosyllables	One of the Narratives next in order after monosyllables in an elementary reading book used in the school.	A short paragraph from an elementary reading book used in the school.
Writing	Form on blackboard or slate from dictation, letters capital and small manuscript.	Copy in manuscript character a line of print.	A sentence from the same paragraph, slowly read once, and then dictated in single words.
Arithmetic	Form on blackboard or slate, from dictation, figures up to 20: name at sight figures up to 20: add and subtract figures up to 10, orally, and from examples on blackboard.	A sum in simple addition and subtraction, and the multiplication table.	A sum in any simple rule as far as short division (inclusive).

	IV	V	VI
Reading	A short paragraph from a more advanced reading book used in the school.	A few lines of poetry from a reading book used in the first class in the school.	A short ordinary paragraph in a newspaper, or other modern narrative.
Writing	A sentence slowly dictated once by a few words at a time from the same book, but not from the paragraph read.	A sentence slowly dictated once, by a few words at a time, from a reading book used in the first class of the school.	Another short ordinary paragraph in a newspaper, or other modern narrative, slowly dictated once by a few words at a time.
Arithmetic	A sum in compound rules (money).	A sum in compound rules (common weights and measures.)	A sum in practice or bills of parcels.

A seventh standard was added in 1882.

Though voluntary schools invariably provided religious instruction some school boards did not. Thus from 1873 in Birmingham arrangements were made for teachers from the Religious Education Society to use the school premises for an hour on two days per week to provide religious teaching only for those pupils whose parents wished it.

In the 1870s the teaching of subjects other than the 3Rs was encouraged by a further range of grants from the central government. 'Class' subjects — grammar, history, geography, plain needlework — were to be taken by a whole class. Other grants for 'specific' subjects, to be taken by individuals, were made for English Literature, mathematics, French, German, Latin, mechanics, botany, and other seemingly esoteric studies. Some pupils were presented for the even higher standards, and grant payments, of the Science and Art examinations. The Code of 1890 acknowledged the importance of physical education. Science and other subjects, manual training, physical education, singing and the like, might involve considerable capital expenditure and occasion much controversy. For example, pianos became a crucial issue in the London School Board election of 1891.

Payment by results was abolished in 1897 and other piecemeal grants in 1900. By that date the curricula of some elementary schools was very different from what it had been in 1870. For example in 1903 all children in London board schools received teaching in history and geography, whilst nearly ten per cent learned French.[34] In addition, particularly in urban areas, a range of activities had grown up around the schools. These included evening associations and classes, school dinners, day excursions and longer holidays, vacation schools, sports facilities and contests.

By the end of the century the larger school boards had significantly modified the former concept of elementary schooling in terms of buildings, equipment and curricula. In some instances higher classes, higher tops, even separate higher grade schools were established for abler pupils. In addition from 1890 a new type of evening school was developed which provided, under school board auspices, more advanced education for young persons and adults.

Traditional basic education in England and Wales had been concerned with matters of religion, occupation, and, to a lesser extent, of literacy. It had been appropriate for people of all ages, from infancy to dotage, and had been undertaken in a variety of situations by a variety of persons. Basic or elementary education as redefined in the years 1870–1900 was a compulsory, age-specific, professional teacher directed, school-based exercise aimed at the mastery of prescribed school subjects grouped around a central core of basic literacy. This definition was confirmed by the Cockerton judgements of 1900–1 which disallowed expenditure by the London School Board on the North London School of Art on the grounds that it was neither elementary instruction nor for children. This decision sealed the fate of the school boards and of their higher grade and evening schools which were deemed to have strayed into the preserves of secondary and higher education. At the same time it strengthened the primary role of elementary schooling, and the ideal of the ladder of opportunity. Prior to 1900 several elementary schools, for example Fleet Road Board School, Hampstead, the 'Eton for nothing a week', had acquired a reputation for preparing pupils for the scholarship examinations of grammar schools. Children from the middling classes had been attracted thereby. The Elementary Code of 1904 confirmed that one important function of elementary schools was 'to discover individual children who show promise of exceptional capacity, and to develop their special gifts (so far as this can be done without sacrificing the interests of the majority of the children), so that they may be qualified to pass at the proper age into Secondary Schools, and be able to derive the maximum of benefit from the education there offered them'.[35]

A 'New' Education

In the years 1905 to 1914 Liberal governments headed by Campbell Bannerman and Asquith laid the foundations of the modern welfare state. Attitudes to poverty and pauperism were changed. The central government assumed a greater responsibility for many sectors of society — labour exchanges, and unemployment and health insurance for the workers, pensions for the elderly. In 1906 an Education (Provision of Meals) Act enabled local authorities to supply school meals, and in 1914 such provision could be extended to the school holidays, an important consideration in wartime conditions. There were frequent complaints that the new LEAs were less active in exercising these powers than the old school boards might have been. In 1907 a medical branch of the Board of Education was set up with George Newman at its head. Local authorities were required to conduct school medical examinations. School milk was introduced in the 1930s when the effects of depression and unemployment led to renewed concern about the extent of malnutrition and deficiency diseases amongst the nation's children. By 1971 health had improved to the extent that school milk was withdrawn, except from infant and special schools.

Attention to the physical well-being of children was but one aspect of the 'New Education' movements of the early twentieth century. A new concern for the 'pre-school child' was particularly important at a time when the concept of age-specific education was leading to the systematic exclusion of the under fives from elementary schools. In 1900 some 43 per cent of the three and four year olds in England and Wales attended elementary schools. By 1930 the figure had been reduced to 13 per cent.[36] Margaret McMillan had experienced slum conditions in Bradford and in the East End of London in her work for the Independent Labour Party. She campaigned vigorously for medical inspection, child clinics, nursery, camp and open air schools, and opened an experimental clinic at Bow in 1908. Her goal was a nursery and infant school system capable of providing for the physical, emotional and mental needs of the younger child.

In London McMillan joined the Froebel Society which, though

reliant upon private finance until 1919, opened free kindergartens in poverty-stricken and deprived areas of many large towns. Another foreign inspiration became available in 1912 with the publication of the first English edition of *The Montessori Method*. It described the use of didactic materials to promote the sensory-motor development of the pre-school child as practised by Maria Montessori, a doctor and psychologist, in the Casa dei Bambini in Rome. In 1919 when Montessori first visited England she was accorded a triumphant welcome.

The prefatory memorandum to the *Handbook of Suggestions for the Consideration of Teachers and others concerned in the work of Public Elementary Schools* (1905) seemed to encourage a new spirit of independence within the elementary school. It declared that 'The only uniformity of practice that the Board of Education desires to see in the teaching of Public Elementary Schools is that each teacher shall think for himself, and work out for himself such methods of teaching as may use his powers to the best advantage and be best suited to the particular needs and conditions of the school'.

This freedom, or uncertainty, proceeding from official quarters, was further highlighted in 1911 when Edmond Holmes,[37] former chief inspector of the Board of Education, in *What Is and What Might Be* called for nothing less than a total revolution inside the elementary school. In the first part of the book, subtitled 'The Path of Mechanical Obedience', Holmes deplored the prevailing system of class teaching which assumed children to be inherently sinful and directed their every thought, word and deed. In the second part, 'The Path of Self-Realisation', Holmes described his ideal school, 'Utopia', and its ideal teacher, 'Egeria'. The school at Sompting in Sussex and its teacher Harriet Finlay-Johnson, which had so captivated Holmes' poetic and romantic mind, were dedicated to the development of initiative and intelligence. The school was characterised in Holmes' opinion by 'the ceaseless activity of the children' and 'the bright and happy look on every face'. The book went through four impressions in seven months and was to inspire a generation of reformist teachers including H. Caldwell Cook whose book *The Play Way* was published in 1917.

In the inter-war years the cause of child-centred education progressed to the extent that by 1939 it had become the intellectual orthodoxy of the primary school and of the training college. An important role in this development was played by Susan Isaacs, a psychologist, who in 1933 became head of the newly-formed

Department of Child Development at the London University Institute of Education. *Intellectual Growth in Young Children* (1930) and *Social Development in Young Children* (1933) drew upon her research at the Malting House Garden School in Cambridge and became prescribed reading for progressive primary educationists.

The primary school

In the harsh reality of post-war demobilisation and unemployment the Fisher Act of 1918 took the opportunity of raising the school leaving age to fourteen and of abolishing all exemptions, thus ending the half-time system. Employment of children under 12 was prohibited, and those between 12 and 14 were restricted to a maximum of two hours per day. LEAs were empowered to establish nursery schools, but this and other provisions, including part time day continuation schooling to 16, fell victim to the financial stringency epitomised by the 'Geddes[38] axe' of 1922.

Sir Henry Hadow, vice-chancellor of Sheffield University, was from 1920 to 1934 chairman of the Board of Education's Consultative Committee. The Hadow report of 1926, *The Education of the Adolescent,* recommended the institution of secondary education for all children with a minimum leaving age of 15, though in different types of post-primary or secondary schools. This would necessitate the abolition of elementary schooling for which the committee proposed to substitute 'the term "primary" but to restrict the use of that term to the period of education which ends at the age of eleven or twelve'. Thus the report of 1931 was entitled *The Primary School* and advised that the curriculum of such a school might include less 'subject' and more 'topic' work and was 'to be thought of in terms of activity and experience rather than of knowledge to be acquired and facts to be stored'. The experience of seventy years, however, was not easily put aside, especially as selection for secondary schooling was usually based upon an examination in the traditional subjects. The report advised that it was 'essential that provision should be made for an adequate amount of "drill" in reading, writing and arithmetic', and warned against relying in matters of selection upon intelligence tests alone. The report of 1933 on *Infant and Nursery Schools* reflected the trends in infant education in the inter-war period. Both Isaacs and Montessori were consulted by the committee.

The Education Act of 1944 confirmed the basic doctrines of the Hadow reports. Elementary schooling disappeared, to be replaced by a continuous formal educational process in three stages — primary, secondary and further. Parents were no longer required by law to ensure that a child received 'efficient elementary instruction in reading, writing and arithmetic', but rather 'efficient full-time education suitable to his age, ability and aptitude'. Religious instruction and a daily corporate act of worship became compulsory in primary and secondary schools.

One universal purpose of basic education thus became to fit children, aged five to eleven years, for the next stage of formal education. This received particular expression in the selection process known as the eleven plus examination, which in some instances resulted in streaming[39] according to academic ability being extended into the infant school. Surveys of 1962 and 1964 showed that 85 per cent of primary teachers and two-thirds of parents favoured streaming. In addition the physical and emotional dimensions of education had been highlighted again during wartime. School meal provision trebled during the Second World War and by 1945 there were some 80 child guidance clinics, the first having been opened in Birmingham in 1932.

Post-war 'baby booms' led to the 'bulges' which passed into the educational system in the 1950s and 1960s, when there were over four million children in primary schools in England and Wales. In consequence the target of a maximum sized primary class of forty children remained a target only in some areas until the 1970s. This was a far cry from the Malting House Garden School where Isaacs had worked with children with an average IQ of 130 in groups of five pupils per teacher. Primary schools in this period exhibited a wide variety of buildings, facilities and teaching methods. In some classrooms serried rows of desks and formal methods of instruction continued. In others, groups of tables, open-plan areas, integrated day and 'modern maths' became the norm. This spectrum was revealed by the Plowden Committee which reported in 1967 on all aspects of English primary education and the transition to the secondary stage. Its Welsh counterpart, the Gittins Report, was issued in the following year.

At a time of great change and expansion in secondary and higher education the Plowden Report brought to public attention the neglect of primary schools in such matters as buildings, equipment and staffing ratios. All but 676 of the 20,664 primary schools in England were surveyed by inspectors, and classified into 9 grades of competence. Category 6 was the largest, with 28 per cent of children. Only 1 per cent were in schools of the first category and only a further 9 per cent in the second, described as 'A good school with some outstanding features'.

The very title of the report, *Children and their Primary Schools*, however, and the child-centred assumptions in its pages, provided a new focus for the debate over formal versus informal methods of instruction. Good schools for Plowden were schools in which children were 'to be themselves' and to live 'as children and not as future adults'. They were to lay 'special stress on individual discovery' and teach 'that knowledge does not fall into neatly separate compartments'. Such views were to be questioned in 1969 by R.S. Peters and in the first two 'Black Papers'.[40] At the same time the doctrines of 'reading readiness' and 'proceeding at the child's own pace' were being modified by the findings of a National Foundation for Educational Research (NFER) study of 1966 which showed that children unable to read by the age of eight were likely to remain backward.

A survey of 37 primary school teachers and their pupils in 1973 and 1974 by Neville Bennett[41] concluded that children taught by formal methods were three to five months ahead in maths and English of those taught by informal means. A government discussion document of 1977 advised that in respect of basic skills in primary schools it was necessary 'to restore the rigour without damaging the real benefits of the child-centred developments'.

In the 1930s the Hadow reports had suggested a demarcation between infants and juniors at seven years of age. The Plowden Report recommended nursery provision from three to five, first schools from five to eight and middle schools from eight to twelve, thus extending the 'age of childhood' and delaying the transfer to secondary schooling. Whatever the rationalisation for this change, and the theories of Piaget underlie much of the report, one effect of this recommendation was to add further variety to the school system. Some authorities provided middle schools for eight to twelve, others from nine to thirteen, others again retained transfer at eleven. Though the ideal of pre-school provision for all children whose parents desired it was taken up by a White Paper of 1972, provision remained patchy, and included a high proportion of privately-organised fee-paying play groups in more affluent areas.

The Plowden Report drew particular attention to what it designated Educational Priority Areas (EPAs). Whereas in the 1860s, in spite of arguments to the contrary, government financial aid had been given to the wealthier areas, it was now agreed that positive discrimination should be made in favour of children in deprived areas. These were to be identified by the high proportions of parents in unskilled jobs, by the large size of family, the recourse to supplementary benefits, the high proportions of children unable to speak English, the overcrowding of housing, and the high incidence of truancy and delinquency. This concern for neighbourhoods which had 'for generations been starved of new schools, new houses and new investment of every kind' was reflected in the speedy designation of EPAs and the allocation of extra money for buildings, staffing and salary supplementation.

Conclusion

By the mid 1970s, however, in England and Wales as in the USA confidence in the ability of positive discrimination in primary schooling alone to break the cycle of deprivation had much diminished. This was hardly surprising. In the perspective of history primary or fundamental education can be seen as a preparation for life in this world and the next which has encompassed church, home and workplace as well as school, adults and young persons as well as children. The nineteenth century provided a more precise form of fundamental education by means of the compulsory schooling of young children. The twentieth-century primary school is even more circumscribed and prepares children for a further or secondary period of schooling rather than for direct entry into the adult world.

The primary schools of England and Wales have rightly achieved a considerable international reputation, particularly in progressive educational circles. To provide basic literacy and other educational and social skills in a happy and secure environment is indeed a worthwhile aim. To give a guarantee of childhood, when the ideal of childhood is under assault, not least from television, is a principle to be upheld. These, however, are but parts of the historical dimensions of basic or primary education.

NOTES

1 **A.F. Leach,** *Educational Charters and Documents* (1911, reprinted 1971), p. 35. This is still the most important collection for the

medieval period.

2 **Leach** (1911), pp. 34, 138.

3 **Leach** (1911), p. 236.

4 **N. Orme,** *Education in the West of England 1066–1548* (1976), p. 3.

5 **Leach** (1911), p. 472.

6 **J.H. Moran,** *Education and Learning in the City of York 1300–1560* (1979), p. 15.

7 **Leach** (1911), p. xiii.

8 **Leach** (1911), p. 424.

9 **Leach** (1911), p. 434.

10 **N. Orme,** *English Schools in the Middle Ages* (1973), p. 61.

11 **Sylvester** (1970), pp. 17–18.

12 **Cressy** (1975), p. 17.

13 **J. Simon,** *Education and Society in Tudor England* (1966), p. 370.

14 **John Milton** (1608–74), poet and supporter of the parliamentary cause.

15 *See* **M.G. Jones,** *The Charity School Movement* (1938, reprinted 1964), and J. Simon, 'Was there a Charity School Movement? The Leicestershire Evidence' in B. Simon (ed.), *Education in Leicestershire 1540–1940* (1968).

16 **Sylvester** (1970), p. 180.

17 **Daniel Defoe** (1660–1731), journalist, political writer and author of *Robinson Crusoe* (1719).

18 **Jones** (1938), p. 89.

19 **Laqueur** (1976), p. 152.

20 **Laqueur** (1976), pp. 44, 246.

21 **Robert Raikes** (1735–1811), proprietor of the *Gloucester Journal*.

22 Quoted in Jones (1938), p. 146.

23 For this debate *see* **Thompson** (1963), Laqueur (1976), and Dick (1980).

24 **Maclure** (1979), p. 26.

25 These proposals proceeded from Whig, Liberal and Radical members of the House of Commons. Fear of tyranny, denominational rivalry and the sheer cost were sufficient to ensure their defeat.

26 **Less eligibility** required that the lot of the pauper in the workhouse should be worse than that of the poorest free labourer outside it.

27 **Parliamentary Papers (hereafter P.P.) 1861, xxi,** *Report of the Commissioners appointed to inquire into the State of Popular Education in England.*

28 **S. Frith** 'Socialization and rational schooling: elementary education in Leeds before 1870', in P. McCann (ed.), *Popular Education and Socialization in the Nineteenth Century* (1977), p. 74.

29 **D. Rubinstein,** 'Socialization and the London School Board 1870–1904: aims, methods and public opinion', in McCann (1977), p. 232.

30 **D. Rubinstein,** *School Attendance in London 1870–1904: a social*

history (1969), p. 112.

31 **J.M. Goldstrom,** *Education: Elementary Education 1780–1900* (1972), pp. 156–7.

32 **Rubinstein** (1969), pp. 112–4.

33 **Maclure** (1979), p. 80.

34 **Rubinstein** in McCann (1977), p. 253.

35 **Maclure** (1979), pp. 154–5.

36 Figures quoted in N. Whitbread, *The Evolution of the Nursery-Infant School* (1972), p. 68.

37 **Edmond Holmes** (1850–1936), HMI 1875–1905, and Chief Inspector of elementary schools 1905–11.

38 **Sir Eric Geddes** was chairman of the Committee on National Expenditure.

39 For the transition from 'standards' to 'streaming' see B. Simon, *The Politics of Educational Reform 1920–1940* (1974), pp. 225–50.

40 *Fight for Education* and *The Crisis in Education* appeared in 1969, *Goodbye Mr Short* in 1970. R.S. Peters (ed.), *Perspectives on Plowden* (1969).

41 **N. Bennett** *et al., Teaching Styles and Pupil Progress* (1976).

5 Secondary Education

Medieval Origins

Vocational training

Some members of medieval society needed a secondary or further education beyond the fundamental learning related to matters of this world and the next. This secondary education was essentially vocational in nature, though it might also entail more general social, cultural and religious dimensions.

The medieval period was one in which kings regularly led their armies on the battlefield, and education for feudal leadership took place in the household and on the hunting and tournament fields. Boys, and some girls, having received a basic instruction at home, would by participating in the workings of a royal or noble household, acquire the managerial and social skills appropriate to their status in life. Such an establishment might also include a chaplain or secular master charged with the duty of giving formal instruction in reading and grammar. From the age of fourteen the former page would, as a squire, pay less attention to household duties, and more to those of military prowess.

The vocational element is most clearly seen in the system of craft apprenticeship as it existed from the thirteenth century. Boys, and less frequently girls, were bound for a period of some seven years from about the age of fourteen during which time they learned not only the mysteries of their craft but also the associated educational, social and religious skills and responsibilities. Similarly boys and young men dedicated to the monastic life, either as oblates by their parents, or as postulants by their own choice, would be schooled to their new life within the cloister walls. For them, as for those other aspirants to the clerical profession who were not under monastic vows, it was essential to learn a second language, namely Latin, the language of the church.

These specifically vocational systems also provided more general educational facilities. Thus some gilds maintained grammar schools not only to assist in the education of apprentices, but also for the children of their masters and others. Monasteries might also provide some secondary education, either by means of chaplain or paid schoolmaster for sons of the wealthy boarded out in the abbot's household, or in an almonry school for poor boys outside the monastery gate. Similarly nunneries provided schooling not only for their novices but also for other daughters from affluent backgrounds and even for their younger brothers. Thus in the early fourteenth century the priory of Benedictine nuns at Amesbury in Wiltshire boarded children of noble birth, including Eleanor the daughter of Edward I, and several children of Isabel, daughter of Henry, Earl of Lancaster.[1]

Subjects of study were those appropriate to young gentlewomen — religion, duty, social accomplishments and reading in English. Latin was less frequently available, and French in the later Middle Ages often only in local dialect form as with Chaucer's Prioress 'after the scole at Stratford atte Bowe'.

The grammar school

The most distinctive form of secondary education to emerge from the medieval period was that of a school whose overriding purpose was to teach Latin — the grammar school. Such schools also had a vocational origin; to train native English speakers in Latin, the language of classical learning and of the Christian faith and church. An early school of this type was at Canterbury. From 597 it was used by St Augustine and his missionary band for the training of priests.

The subjects of study inherited from the Romano-Greek culture of the ancient world formed the background to the curriculum of the medieval period. The seven liberal arts comprised the *trivium* — grammar, logic and rhetoric, and the *quadrivium* — arithmetic, astronomy, geometry and music. In theory the *trivium* formed the basis of secondary education, the *quadrivium* that of higher study. In practice, particularly prior to the thirteenth century, there were considerable overlaps. Thus many grammar schools supplied preliminary instruction in reading and song, whilst Oxford was a leading centre for the study of grammar, and the university arts course also included advanced study of the subject. By the end of the medieval period, however, logic and rhetoric were university subjects, whilst many grammar schools were shedding their elementary functions or assigning such teaching to an under master or usher.

Generalisations about the nature, extent and continuity of medieval grammar schools are fraught with difficulty. Evidence is scanty, often a single reference to a schoolmaster or bequest in a lease or will. Even where fuller details are given there is no way of knowing whether such examples are typical.

Nevertheless it can be stated with some certainty that grammar schools were essentially for boys, who were usually taught in one room, with a chair or desk for the master and benches or the floor for the scholars. Numbers of pupils varied considerably, from small groups in single figures to well over a hundred — for example an estimated maximum of some 150 at St Peter's School, York, in the later fourteenth century.[2] Schools of such size might well have necessitated the employment of an assistant master, and some elements of mutual instruction amongst the pupils themselves. Schoolmasters included priests, clerks and laymen. For example in 1432 the will of William Sevenoaks, a citizen and grocer of London, provided for the maintenance of 'one Master, an honest man, sufficiently advanced and expert in the science of grammar, B.A., by no means in holy orders, to keep a Grammar School in some convenient house within the said town of Sevenoaks'.[3]

Not all grammar school masters were graduates, however, for grammar was only one part of the university arts course, indeed even in the fifteenth and early sixteenth centuries graduates were in the minority. Their position in the social hierarchy was a modest one, certainly below that of a beneficed clergyman or rector, but equal to or above that of a mere curate or chantry priest.

The social origins, expectations and achievements of grammar school pupils are even more difficult to categorise. Schoolboys were tonsured[4] at least until the fourteenth century, but we do not know what proportions completed the grammar school course or used their Latin in clerical as opposed to lay occupations, if at all. In many schools, as at Sevenoaks, the master was required 'to teach and instruct all poor boys whatsoever coming there for the sake of learning, taking nothing of them or their parents or friends'.[5] In cathedral grammar schools, however, the master customarily took in fee-paying pupils as well. This was the practice at Winchester where in addition to the original 70 poor scholars there were non-foundationers — fee-paying boarders of noble or wealthy origin. Similarly the free grammar school of Eton, founded originally in 1440 by Henry VI for 25 poor and needy scholars (a number soon increased to 70), also attracted fee-paying sons of the nobility and gentry. Eton soon became, as its founder had intended, a 'public and general grammar school, and that the same school as it surpasses all other such grammar schools whatsoever of our kingdom in the affluence of its endowment and the pre-excellence of its foundation, so it may excel all other grammar schools, as it ought, in the prerogative of its name'.[6]

The grammar school day was long, possibly ten hours or more, starting at six in the morning, six days a week. Holidays were based on religious and local custom. Statutes of the free grammar school founded in 1384 at Wotton under Edge in Gloucestershire by Lady Katherine Berkeley, laid down in perpetuity a pattern of school holidays remarkably similar to those of today. There were two weeks at Easter and one at Whitsun. The summer holiday was from 1 August to 14 September, and at Christmas from 21 December to 7 January.[7]

Latin

Latin was the purpose of grammar school study — its speaking, reading and writing — and was naturally spoken in school at every opportunity. From the conquest until the middle of the fourteenth century French was used as the vernacular, but John Cornwall a master of grammar at Merton College School, Oxford, is credited with having restored the practice of translating from and into English.

> ... so that now, the year of our Lord a thousand three hundred four score and five, and of the second king Richard after the conquest nine, in all the grammar schools of England, children leave French and construe and learn in English...
>
> Their advantage is that they learn their grammar in less time than children were wont to do; the disadvantage is that now children of grammar school know no more French than can their left heel, and that is harm for them and they shall pass the sea and travel in strange lands and in many other places.[8]

The *Ars Minor* (c.350) of Aelius Donatus, a book so widely used that grammar school pupils or those in the younger forms were sometimes referred to as 'donats' or 'donatists', was the standard elementary Latin grammar of the medieval period. More advanced works included the *Ars Major* of Priscian which dated from the fifth century, and the *Doctrinale* (c. 1200) of Alexander de Villa Dei of Brittany. These works underwent various revisions and reformulations, whilst some grammar masters produced their own manuscripts by adapting the well-known texts for their particular purposes. Aesop's *Fables* and the *Distichs* of Cato were popular examples of the many works of maxims, precepts, fables and proverbs employed as reading books. The *Catholicon* (*c.* 1285) of John of Genoa included alphabetical lists of Latin words with meanings, though these too were given in Latin. From the fifteenth century a new breed of dictionaries like the *Medulla Grammatice* gave English meanings of Latin words.

Shortages of books and of writing materials necessitated the use of dictation, recitation, learning by rote and learning by heart. To assist this process many works, including the *Doctrinale*, were written in verse. The popularity of this grammar treatise of some 2,650 hexameters is shown by the appearances of more than 260 editions between 1470 and the 1520s.[9]

Sixteenth to Eighteenth Centuries

Household and apprenticeship

Household education continued into the early modern period for children of the nobility, and was particularly favoured by Catholic families after the Reformation. Though military and courtly skills had an important place in the Renaissance ideal, in practice their utility declined. By the seventeenth century boys would no longer be placed under the care of a master of the henchmen but rather in the company of a learned tutor.

The royal household remained paramount, and doubtless gave some encouragement to the education of girls during the reigns of the Tudor queens. Sir William Cecil, Secretary of State to Queen Elizabeth and Chancellor of the University of Cambridge, was, from 1561 in his capacity as Master of the Court of Wards, responsible for supervising the upbringing of orphaned sons of noble birth. Cecil House in the Strand was an elite establishment concentrating upon those whose inheritance was in excess of £1,000, and including the Earls of Essex, Oxford, Rutland, Southampton and Surrey. Instruction was given in writing, drawing, Latin, French, riding, shooting, dancing and other skills.[10]

In the seventeenth century John Locke, himself for a time a tutor in the household of the Earl of Shaftesbury, advised gentlemen to educate their sons at home by means of a private tutor, rather than submit them to the physical, moral and mental torments of a grammar or great school. Indeed, though home and school were not mutually exclusive educational agencies, life in a great household had considerable advantages, not least for the tutor. A fine library, works of art, scientific and curio collections, extensive grounds and informed and influential company clustered around an hospitable table, might well provide a more conducive educational setting than school, academy or university. Daniel Defoe criticised Newington Green Academy for its want of conversation. Joseph Priestley, after teaching at Warrington Academy,[11] in the 1770s became tutor and librarian to the household of the Earl of Shelburne.

Similarly in the sixteenth century the apprenticeship system continued to supply commercial, technical and general education in a household context. Entry was controlled in several ways. For example by 1478 the Goldsmiths' Company required that none should be apprenticed who could not read and write.[12] In other cases further basic schooling in English, and occasionally Latin if required, would be incorporated into the apprenticeship agreement. Entry to some elite occupations, particularly in London, was further restricted in a social sense. The commercial aristocracy of the capital was not to be recruited from amongst the sons of landless labourers, but rather from the offspring of men of property, though much of it newly acquired.

Private schools and academies

Social changes of the sixteenth century — the rise in population, the rise of the gentry, the rise of the scholar statesman — none of which was an exclusively Tudor phenomenon, had important implications for schooling as the second stage of education. Some of the dimensions are impossible to quantify. Freelance teachers and teaching, both clerical and lay, existed in the sixteenth, seventeenth and eighteenth centuries, as in the fifteenth. Their importance is easily neglected for their transient activities and establishments have left few records. In official compilations they frequently appear as villains of the piece, over whom officials of church and state sought to exercise their powers to license and control. Their schools, conducted in a variety of situations, but dependent upon the fees charged, are equally impossible to classify. They have been termed 'private' to distinguish them from the more 'public' grammar or endowed schools.

In 1951 Nicholas Hans attempted to divide the superior private schools of the eighteenth century into two broad categories — the classical and the modern.[13]

Private classical schools were frequently those kept by Anglican clergymen, resident and non-resident, who boarded and taught a number of boys in parsonage or private house. For example the first headmaster of Cheam School was George Aldrich, himself educated at Westminster and Trinity College, Cambridge, and from 1644 curate of Crowhurst. Cheam opened in the following year and in 1650 two of its pupils were admitted to Cambridge. In the eighteenth century boys continued to pass directly to the universities. In the second half of the nineteenth Cheam became a preparatory for the public schools.

Modern schools or academies were more frequently owned and taught by non-graduate laymen. Some catered for the gentry and provided a broad literary and scientific education. Hackney Academy was the most famous example of this type, founded about 1685 by Benjamin Morland, and enjoying an uninterrupted existence until 1820. In 1721 Morland was appointed high master of St Paul's, and Hackney in the hands of the Newcome family became a school for sons of the aristocracy and the wealthy. Scores of its pupils proceeded directly to university, having experienced a six year course which offered classical and modern languages, maths, science, physical education and the accomplishments of drawing, dancing and music.

Other academies placed greater emphasis upon preparation for military, naval, business or trade careers. Whereas curricula and teaching methods in the grammar schools were still often fettered by trust deed, statute and custom, modern academies were able to respond to the educational and vocational needs of a more commercial and industrial society. Thus the naval academy founded in Chelsea in 1782 by John Bettesworth offered instruction relevant to the counting house, public offices and trade. Its prime purpose, however, was to prepare the sons of gentlemen for a naval career. A ship, the *Cumberland*, fully rigged and mounted on swivels was erected in the playground, whilst other school equipment included a rope house and a battery of six pounders.

Girls' education

Private establishments, moreover, provided the major means for the schooling of girls from the upper reaches of society, particularly after the dissolution of the nunneries. Neither Renaissance, Reformation, humanism, a civil war, nor two Tudor queens, one of whom was the Supreme Governor of the Anglican church, could break the male monopoly of the religious, professional, political and business worlds. In consequence writers upon female education like Thomas Becon in 1559 advocated schoolmistresses and schooling for girls essentially for reducing the ranks of 'idle, unhonest and lewd women', and 'to bring up the maids and young women in the doctrine and nurture of the Lord'.[14] Similarly Richard Mulcaster wrote in 1581 of educating girls not in grammar schools or universities, 'because naturally the male is more worthy and politically he is more employed', but with due regard to the 'difference of their calling'.[15]

Girls, therefore, continued to be educated at home; by parents, other relations, governesses and tutors, or in private day or boarding schools. Moral education, and accomplishments, particularly French, music, dancing, drawing and needlework constituted the basic curriculum. The main purpose of this education was to produce good daughters, many of whom would ultimately become good wives. By the end of the eighteenth century, however, several writers, including Erasmus Darwin, Mary Wollstonecraft, and Hester Chapone, were presenting the case for a broader range of studies, more akin to that of the best modern academies.

Grammar schools

The sixteenth and seventeenth centuries saw the foundation or refoundation of large numbers of endowed grammar schools, many of which included some provision for free schooling. In Henry VIII's reign, following the dissolution of the monasteries, an Act of 1540 reconstituted the monastic cathedrals and prescribed in detail the form of new King's schools as at Canterbury, Ely, Rochester and Worcester. In the next two years other King's schools were established where former abbey churches were elevated to cathedral rank, as at Chester, Gloucester and Peterborough.[16] In the later 1540s suppression of colleges of priests, chantries and chapels led to the refoundation of some educational establishments, often as King Edward VI grammar schools. Limitations in our knowledge of the precise extent of schooling immediately prior to the Reformation, however, make it impossible to compile an accurate profit and loss account.

Three of the great grammar schools of the sixteenth century were founded in London. These were St Paul's, whose first high master William Lily took office in 1510 with a stipend of £35 and who together with an usher was to teach some 150 boys without charge. This school, the prototype of humanist learning, attracted the support of Erasmus. It was placed under the control of the Mercers' company, the city company of the father of its founder, Dean Colet. Westminster, refounded in 1560 by Queen Elizabeth, was intended for 120 boys in the charge of two masters. The Merchant Taylors' School, established in the next year, followed closely upon the statutes of St Paul's, and provided for 250 pupils, of whom 100 would be admitted without charge. More modest schools were founded in market towns throughout the country. It has been estimated that in the years 1558–1685 at least 358 new grammar schools were founded; 136 in the reign of Elizabeth, 83 in the time of James I, 59 under Charles I, and 80 under Charles II.[17]

Many of the features of the medieval grammar schools continued into the early modern period — the single schoolroom, the one master, perhaps assisted by an usher, the long school day, the use of corporal punishment. The licensing of schoolmasters, though by bishops rather than by cathedral chancellors, reintroduced in the reign of Mary for the purpose of confirming the Catholic faith, was continued by her successors in the cause of protestantism. Schoolmasters were required to teach the catechism and to convey their pupils to church to attend the sermon. Even textbooks were standardised anew on royal authority. Thus the works of John Stanbridge, Master at Magdalen College School, Oxford, from 1488–94 and his pupil Robert Whittinton who became master at the hospital at Lichfield, fell into disfavour and were replaced in 1540–2 by the *Royal Grammar* based on the writings of Erasmus, Colet and Lily. Various manuals, Roger Ascham's *The Scholemaster,* published posthumously in 1570, Richard Mulcaster's, *Positions* (1581), John Brinsley's, *Ludus Literarius, or The Grammar Schoole* (1612) and Charles Hoole's, *A New Discovery of the Old Art of Teaching Schoole* (1660), gave advice on teaching method. Boys were to begin by learning the rules of Latin grammar, and by 'making Latins', often involving a double translation, first from Latin into English, and then, after some time had elapsed, by retranslation into Latin. These skills having been acquired, pupils would be set to Latin composition, firstly in imitation of classical authors with whose works they were familiar, and finally in their

own independent style. The statutes of some schools provided that
only Latin, or exceptionally Latin or Greek, should be spoken in
school. In the sixteenth century Greek, and to a lesser extent
Hebrew, entered the curriculum of some schools, but in the
majority Latin remained the essential subject of study.

Other dimensions of grammar schooling are more difficult to
determine with precision. Age of admission varied, probably
between seven and twelve years, whilst the minority who proceeded
to university did so in their middle or later teens.[18] We do not know
what proportion of schoolmasters had recourse to other duties to
supplement their incomes, or taught petty or other subjects. We do
not know how many pupils stayed the full course, or paid fees, or
boarded, nor how many schools admitted girls. Social origins of
pupils are unclear, although grammar schools undoubtedly
contained higher proportions of the sons of the upper and middling
ranks of society than of the poorest labourers. Schooling was seen
by many as a means of reinforcing the social order, by others as a
way of allowing at least some social mobility. Thus in 1540, during
the reorganisation of the cathedral school at Canterbury, Archbishop
Cranmer argued, 'Wherefore if the gentleman's son be apt to
learning, let him be admitted; if not apt, let the poor man's child
that is apt enter his room'.[19]

The grammar schools have been seen as the favourite charitable
device of the Tudor and Stuart period, as a classic example of the
educational commitment of the age, as an essential means of
gentrification, as a key component in an 'educational revolution'.[20]
On the other hand the value of endowments for grammar schooling
may have been overestimated, and due account has not been given
to the effects of the rapid inflation of the period.[21] Uniformity in
the matters of school statutes, doctrinal observance, text books and
teaching methods must on occasion have produced a stultifying
effect, and an education which reflected neither the best ideals of
renaissance humanism nor the needs of the local community. In
1611 Francis Bacon warned James I that the state was oversupplied
with scholars for whom there was no suitable employment, but
short of husbandmen and trade apprentices. He concluded 'that for
grammar schools there are already too many'.[22] It was widely
believed that such alienated intellectuals, steeped in the classical
traditions of the resistance of assemblies to tyrannical kings, were
the root cause of the civil war, an argument which some like
Christopher Wase in 1678 were still trying to refute on the grounds
that 'a youth brought up at school will be taken apprentice with less

money than one illiterate'.[23] Control of grammar school masters continued during the interregnum. Puritan suspicions of grammar schooling centred not only upon the political and religious opinions of their teachers, but also upon the dangerous diet of pagan and 'lewd' authors which classical study entailed.

Estimates of the numbers of post-Restoration grammar schools have varied widely. Christopher Wase's inquiries of the 1670s yielded a list of some 700 in England and Wales, though not all free grammar schools. Though the overall total was probably higher (modern calculations include the 1000 schools of Oakeshott and the 1300 of Vincent)[24] there were perhaps some 6–700 grammar schools functioning at any one time in England and Wales in the late seventeenth and eighteenth centuries. The issue is complicated both by the fragmentary nature of the evidence and by the problems of definition. Joan Simon has suggested that some of the private classical schools listed in Hans' pioneering study *New Trends in Education in the Eighteenth Century* (1951) were in fact endowed grammar schools.[25] Not all endowed schools were grammar schools, however, and the terms 'grammar school', 'free school', 'parish school' and 'public school' were used indiscriminately. Some grammar schools offered free education to all boys in a parish. Others provided a fixed number of free places. Others again offered free places only to the sons of a favoured few — the founders' descendants, the trustees, the subscribers, the burgesses.

Eighteenth-century grammar schools fulfilled a variety of functions, Eton and Westminster were the great schools of the period. Of the forty-seven ministers of state in the last quarter of the eighteenth century at least thirty-four had attended one or other, or even both, of these two schools.[26] Here classical studies reigned supreme, with only minor provision for such extras as French, mathematics, drawing and fencing. Here a boy also learned to survive in a physical and social sense. Fighting, bullying, riots, public affrays, beatings and spartan living conditions were the order of the day. If the Duke of Wellington did indeed remark that the battle of Waterloo was won on the playing fields of Eton he was not simply referring to the practice of organised games. A classical curriculum could be sedulously followed in the great schools and in other large grammar schools which continued regularly to send boys to the universities. Continued adherence to the classics was a hallmark of an emerging great school as at Harrow or Rugby where local grammar schools were deliberately transformed into national institutions by ex-Etonian headmasters who encouraged the boarding of fee-paying pupils of high social status. Other schools flourished in a local context. Hull Grammar School, under the controversial preacher and writer Joseph Milner, headmaster from 1767 to 1797, became 'the great seminary for boys in the East Riding'[27] and sent several pupils to Cambridge. In the years 1749–84, 183 boys, of whom 153 were boarders, proceeded to the universities from Manchester Grammar School. The majority of local day boys, however, would leave between twelve and fourteen and either enter a commercial academy or an apprenticeship.[28] The Royal Mathematical School established at Christ's Hospital in the 1670s was intended to prepare some forty boys for apprenticeship at sea. These, however, were but a small proportion of the Christ's Hospital schools which often totalled 1200 pupils. Other grammar schools were founded in coastal areas for the same purpose, as at Dartmouth in 1679 and Rochester in 1701.

Many endowed grammar schools were small, and had fewer than thirty boys even in the best of times. Decline in the demand for classical teaching and the competition of private schools produced radical responses, many of which were condemned in the nineteenth and twentieth centuries as degradation, and attributed to corruption of various kinds. Some schools closed altogether; others enjoyed an intermittent existence. Some became elementary schools, providing a basic English instruction only. Others diversified. Extra subjects, for which fees could be charged since these were not the 'free' subjects of the foundation, were added and boarding facilities provided. Thus the curriculum of the grammar school at Congleton in Cheshire was widened to include writing, arithmetic, merchants' accounts, French and geography. In 1770 at Woodchurch the master of the grammar school advertised a curriculum which promised (in addition to the classics) arithmetic, bookkeeping, logarithms, geometry, mensuration, gauging, trigonometry, mechanics, surveying, levelling, navigation, geography, natural philosophy, astronomy and the use of globes. Boarders were admitted to both these schools, and by the end of the eighteenth century a boarding education at Congleton cost some forty guineas per year.[29]

Nineteenth and Twentieth Centuries

Public schools

In the first half of the nineteenth century Eton, Winchester, Charterhouse, Harrow, Rugby, Westminster and Shrewsbury, together with two day schools, St Paul's and Merchant Taylors', emerged as the great public schools of England. Their status was confirmed by the terms of reference of the Clarendon Commission which in 1861 investigated these nine schools. By 1900, however, the term 'public school' was being applied in a broader sense. Honey's classification of the public schools of the late nineteenth century by interaction in terms of sporting fixtures showed 'short-lists of twenty-two or fewer schools extending to thirty, fifty or sixty-four schools, or by a long-list of up to one hundred and four schools, with an appendix or fringe of up to sixty schools all of highly questionable public-school standing'.[30] Preparatory schools also proliferated. These numbered 400 by the end of the nineteenth century, and allowed the public schools to concentrate upon the older boys.

The public school explosion of the nineteenth century was a means of conferring or confirming the status of the sons of emergent, professional, middle and upper class groups. Their purpose was to produce manly gentleman as exemplified in the heroes of the Roman Republic. Classics indeed retained its high status and predominance in the public school. The introduction of other subjects was resisted on practical grounds: the conservative curricula of Oxford and Cambridge, the shortage of good teachers, the expense of providing new facilities, particularly for the teaching of science. Moreover a series of widely-held rationalisations had been created. These included the difficulty and irrelevance of classics, grammatical accuracy and precision, mental training, and moral and cultural values. Classical study gave the upper classes in society a common esoteric culture which distinguished them from the middling and lower orders.

Thomas Arnold, who emphasised the moral value of classical study, was but the most famous of many great headmasters of this period. He had no fundamental belief in schooling itself, and was well aware of the dangers of the Rugby over which he presided between 1828 and 1842. He agonised over whether to allow his own four sons to become pupils there. Arnold's reforms stemmed from his determination to stamp out sin and to improve the moral tone of society. In 1831 he himself assumed the chaplaincy of the school. His assistant masters were required to exercise a general pastoral care over the boarding houses, a practice usually more associated with private than with public schools. Sixth formers and prefects were charged with the duty of diffusing religious and moral principles amongst the younger boys. Those who transgressed, even in minor matters, were unhesitatingly expelled, cast out lest they should pollute the ideal of Christian manliness to which Arnold had dedicated his closed, corporate world.

Christian manliness, however, often became muscular Christianity, or sheer muscularity. The rise of the games cult was a most significant feature of the second half of the century. Games helped to canalise aggressive elements in boys, and reduced the long-standing fear of rebellions. In 1863 the rules of Association Football were drawn up at Charterhouse, and in 1880 the Old Carthusians won the Football Association Cup. In 1871 public school old boys founded the Rugby Football Union. Sporting prowess became a basic qualification for entry into Oxford and Cambridge, whilst possession of a 'blue' became a passport to success in a variety of occupations including the teaching profession and the Anglican Church.

Some public schools, like Christ's Hospital, a Tudor boarding school for the poor, were ancient foundations. Others like Wellington College, the nation's memorial to the Iron Duke, and originally intended for the free education of the orphaned sons of army officers, sprang from the heart of the Victorian era. Proprietary schools, established by companies but not for profit, included large day schools like those of King's College and University College, London, and the Anglican boarding schools of the 1840s, Brighton, Cheltenham, Hurstpierpoint, Marlborough and Radley. Marlborough was intended primarily for the sons of Anglican clergy. Caterham was founded in 1811 for the sons of Congregational ministers, Eltham College in 1842 for the sons of missionaries, Epsom in 1853 for the sons of doctors. Cheltenham College, the first major foundation of the Victorian era, was originally intended as a proprietary grammar school for day boys. Each shareholder had the right to nominate a boy to the school. Cheltenham itself was a spa and residential area, particularly popular with retired civil and military officers from the colonial services. Sons of tradesmen were rigorously excluded from the school. A boarding house was opened, and Cheltenham soon obtained national recognition as a public school. In 1877 only 222 of its 676 pupils were day boys. The 'Modern' side at Cheltenham offered such exotic extras as Hindustani and Sanscrit, and enabled boys to follow in their fathers' footsteps as builders of the empire.

In 1864 the report of the Clarendon Commission identified five areas of concern about the public schools. These were: the constitution and powers of governing bodies; the relationship between headmasters and assistants, and between foundation scholars and other boys; the narrowness of the curriculum; and the inadequate organisation and teaching, which produced 'a large proportion of men of idle habits and empty and uncultivated minds'. In spite of these faults, however, the Commissioners concluded:

> It is not easy to estimate the degree in which the English people are indebted to these schools for the qualities on which they pique themselves the most — for their capacity to govern others and control themselves, their aptitude for combining freedom with order, their public spirit, their vigour and manliness of character, their strong but not slavish respect for public opinion, their love of healthy sports and exercise. These schools have been the chief nurseries of our statesmen ... and they have had perhaps the largest share in moulding the character of an English gentleman.[31]

Endowed schools

In 1864 the Schools Inquiry (Taunton) Commission was established to investigate the education given in schools not included in the Newcastle and Clarendon inquiries. The twenty-one volumes provide a wealth of evidence about mid-nineteenth-century schooling, indeed they have been called 'the most complete sociological information pertaining to education ever assembled in this country.'[32] Taunton identified three categories of school — 'endowed', 'proprietary' and 'private'. The endowed schools included over 2,000 which gave elementary instruction, and more than 700 grammar schools. Less than 40 of these, however, regularly sent three or more pupils to Oxford and Cambridge. The grammar schools contained 27,595 day boys and 9,279 boarders, the proprietary schools, 7,400 day and 4,600 boarders. In the third group it was estimated were more than 10,000 private schools run by individuals for profit. Three grades of school were identified. The first was for pupils who would stay until eighteen years of age and try for university. Many proprietary and ambitious grammar schools came into this group. Schools of the second grade would be day schools which offered an education until sixteen years for boys who would enter business, commercial or professional careers. Third-grade schools would keep boys until fourteen only. Though some Latin might be taught such schools were basically for the sons of tradesmen and superior artisans.

The Commissioners concluded that the endowed schools were failing to supply one of the great needs of the country — a good education for the lower section of the middle classes and respectable artisans. Neither the proprietary nor the private schools, they believed, were adequately filling this gap. The Commissioners regretted, moreover, that proprietary schools were 'class schools', devoted only to the interest of one group, and favoured instead the encouragement of talent in all ranks of society: 'We cannot but consider, that it is a matter of national interest, that boys of real ability, in whatever rank of life they may be found, should receive every aid and encouragement that can rightly be given to enable them to rise to a position suitable to their talents'.

Thus the Taunton Commissioners in their Report recommended nothing less than a national system of secondary education. This was to be achieved by several means. The first step was to re-organise and reform existing endowments, and, where possible, extend the provision to girls as well as boys. This recommendation was implemented by the Endowed Schools Act of 1869. Some 235 schemes were prepared before the powers of the Endowed Schools Commissioners were transferred to the Charity Commissioners in 1874. Twenty years later a further 616 schemes had been produced, so that five-sevenths of the available funds had been reorganised. At the same time care was taken to provide a proportion of free or assisted places, so that the principle of an educational ladder was secured. In 1883 the Fortescue Return[33] presented evidence from 166 endowed schools, 20 first grade, 70 second grade and 76 third grade. Ex-elementary school pupils accounted for 9 per cent, 39 per cent and 56 per cent respectively of scholarship holders in these schools. The proportion of free places steadily increased, so that by 1907, *before* the 25 per cent free place regulations of that year, a survey of 600 schools showed that free places stood at 28 per cent. Some 24 per cent of pupils in these schools had previously attended public elementary schools.

For the Taunton Commissioners, however, reorganisation of endowments was but a first step. They concluded that it was impossible to leave secondary education to the charity of pious founders. Their Report proposed local rate aid for school buildings and scholarship provision for the poor, a central agency including a national examining council, and a Teachers' Register. These proposals, if implemented, would have transformed this section of schooling in the last quarter of the nineteenth century, much as the school boards transformed elementary education.

Opposition was considerable. In 1868 state intervention in education was still of a limited nature. The principle of rate aid had not yet been established. The traumas of the Revised Code and payment by results cast a long shadow over the concept of centralised examinations. Opponents included churchmen who feared the secularisation of endowments, the Conservative party who in 1874 killed off the Endowed Schools Commission, and all those headmasters, governors, trustees and parents who resented interference in their own particular schools.

This resentment found particular expression in Edward Thring, headmaster of Uppingham. In 1853 Thring had taken charge of this small country grammar school of some twenty-five boys. Within a few years there were 320 pupils, which Thring considered to be the optimum number. In 1869 he organised opposition to clauses in the Endowed Schools Bill which would have curtailed the powers of headmasters. Thirteen schools were represented in a meeting at Uppingham in December 1869, and from this beginning grew the Headmasters' Conference. Thirty-four schools were represented in 1870, and fifty in 1871 when it was decided to establish an annual conference. By 1902 numbers had risen to more than 100. First grade schools, whether public, endowed or proprietary were admitted.

In 1895 the Bryce Commission[34] reported upon the changes of the past thirty years, and in particular upon the reforms effected in the endowments and management of grammar schools, and in the increased provision of schooling for girls. Many problems remained. There was still a grossly unequal distribution of secondary schooling across the country, although higher grade schools and pupil-teacher centres had provided new dimensions. In spite of the grants of the Science and Art Department, science teaching was still neglected. The Devonshire Commission which reported in 1875 showed that only 63 of the 128 endowed schools from which replies had been received were teaching any science, whilst only 13 were supplied with a laboratory.

Girls and young ladies

In the nineteenth century there was still but little prospect of higher education or professional employment for women, whilst even the opportunities for marriage were in decline. In 1851 there were 8,781,000 men and 9,146,000 women in England and Wales. By 1901 these numbers had risen to 15,729,000 and 16,799,000 respectively. The Taunton Commissioners reported that poor as was the provision for secondary schooling for boys, that for girls was much worse. Many single women sought employment as governesses, and the plight of the genteel governess, required to supply her charges with moral and spiritual guidance, instruction in etiquette, reading, writing, music, singing, dancing, drawing, French and other accomplishments, and all for some £20 per year, was a favourite theme in Victorian novels. The Governesses' Benevolent Institution, founded some two years previously, was reformed in 1843 with Rev. David Laing as its secretary. A register was established and a committee of education formed. Further premises were opened in Harley Street, and in 1848 Queen's College was founded. Professors from King's College, London, provided much of the teaching. The curriculum was broad, and included English, Latin, mathematics, theology, history, geography, modern languages, fine arts and pedagogy. Attendance was not confined to governesses, but open to all ladies over the age of twelve. Amongst the first students were Frances Mary Buss, Dorothea Beale, and Sophia Jex-Blake. It soon became necessary to group the students into seniors and juniors. In 1849 a separate preparatory class was opened for girls aged nine years and over.

Dorothea Beale became a tutor at Queen's, and in 1858, at the age of twenty-seven was appointed principal of the Ladies' College, Cheltenham, the first girls' proprietary school. During her forty-year reign the college developed several dimensions. Numbers of pupils multiplied. The curriculum was broadened to include mathematics, science, Latin and Greek. In 1864 the first official boarding house was opened. By the end of the century Cheltenham Ladies' College had become a unique national institution, a community educating nearly 1,000 girls and young ladies. 'A child, starting in the Kindergarten, could pass through the three Divisions into which the College was divided, ending with work for the BA or BSc degree in Pass or Honours in a department which was recognised as a University College. Miss Beale, as someone put it, "takes pupils from the cradle to the grave".'[35]

In 1850 Frances Buss, another former Queen's student, opened the North London Collegiate School for Ladies in her family's house in Camden Street. Influential helpers were on hand including Laing who had agreed to act as school superintendent and teacher of Scripture. By the end of the first year pupil numbers had risen from 35 to 115. Though some boarders were accommodated, the North London was essentially a day school. Whereas at Cheltenham only girls of the prosperous middle class were accepted, Buss admitted daughters of tradespeople and ordinary workers into her school. She permitted neither social nor religious distinctions.

Emily Davies had been educated at home. After the death of her clergyman father she moved to London where she became friendly with many of the early pioneers of the women's movement, including Elizabeth Garrett, Bessie Parkes and Barbara Leigh Smith. In 1862 she formed a committee for the purpose of securing the admission of girls to university local examinations. Though Oxford and London refused, Cambridge permitted girls to sit for the Local Examination in 1863, with Buss providing twenty-five of the ninety-one candidates. The girls acquitted themselves well in many subjects, particularly in view of the very short time, a mere six weeks, available for preparation. The Cambridge Locals were accordingly opened to girls on equal terms for a trial period of three years, and subsequently on a permanent basis.

In 1864 Davies prepared a paper entitled 'On Secondary Instruction Relating to Girls' which was read to the annual congress of the National Association for the Promotion of Social Science (NAPSS) meeting in September at York. Early in 1865 she was informed that the Taunton Commissioners were 'willing to embrace in their survey the education of both sexes alike'.[36]

In her evidence to the Commisson Davies asserted that endowments which originally had been intended for all the children of a particular locality had been alienated to use for boys alone. Christ's Hospital was a flagrant example. In 1865 there were 1,192 boys and twenty-seven masters, but at the girls' school only eighteen girls and one mistress. She asked for reapplication of endowments to girls' education, and for government financial assistance, not only for buildings but also for scholarships and exhibitions. She also suggested that all public examinations should be opened equally to boys and girls.

Buss in her evidence reiterated the need for endowments and for equal access to examinations. She also gave details of the work of her school — its pupils, curriculum and teaching. She advised that many girls came in a state of great ignorance, and that one of the most fundamental reasons for the poor quality of girls' schools was the lack of trained teachers. Beale gave evidence some five months later in April 1866. She too emphasised the ignorance of girls on admission to the College, and confirmed Buss' judgment that trained teachers in elementary schools provided a more efficient education than that given in girls' private schools.

The achievements of Beale and Buss and their schools were in marked contrast to the general standard of girls' schools as reported on by the assistant commissioners. Their examples, however, together with the performance of girls in the Cambridge Locals, convinced the commissoners that 'the essential capacity for learning is the same, or nearly the same, in the two sexes'. They recommended that 'the education of girls is as much a matter of public concern as that of boys, and one to which charitable funds may properly be applied even when girls are not expressly mentioned in the instrument of foundation'.[37]

The Endowed Schools Act of 1869 implemented this policy. The twelve existing endowed schools were expanded, new schools were founded, and funds set aside for scholarships and exhibitions. The commissioners' broader aim, however, of establishing secondary schools for girls on the model of the North London Collegiate in every town in the country was not immediately achieved. Nevertheless in the years to 1874 new schemes were provided for 178 grammar schools of which forty-seven were for girls and one mixed.[38]

The pioneers redoubled their efforts. In 1869 Davies opened a college at Hitchin in which tuition was given by visiting Cambridge dons. Five years later it moved to Cambridge as Girton College. In 1870 Oxford Local examinations were opened to girls, and in 1878 London University admitted women to degrees.

Though Buss was also a strong supporter of Girton, her main interest was still the school she had founded in 1850. In 1871 it moved to new premises and became a public grammar school as the North London Collegiate School for Girls. At the same time a second school, the Camden School, was established in the former buildings, with its own headmistress and Buss as superintendent. The Camden School had lower fees, a leaving age of sixteen, and a series of scholarships to enable promising pupils to transfer to the North London. The schools of the Girls' Public Day School Company, founded in 1872 largely as the result of the work of the

Women's Educational Union and two sisters, Maria Grey and Emily Shirreff, were modelled on the North London. By the end of the century there were thirty-eight GPDS schools. In 1878 the Maria Grey Training College was established to train their teachers.

Other schools founded on the same principles were the High Schools of the Church Schools Company, and several secondary schools for Roman Catholic girls.

Beale's continuing influence is more clearly seen in the girls' public boarding schools. In 1877 an ex-teacher of Cheltenham who had been one of the original Hitchin students, Louisa Lumsden, became the first headmistress of St Leonard's at St Andrews in Scotland. Roedean was founded in 1885, Wycombe Abbey in 1896 by Jane Dove, Lumsden's successor at St Leonard's. St Felix and Sherborne were opened at the end of the nineteenth century, St Paul's Girls' School, a day school, in 1904. In the same period sister schools were opened to the Woodard Foundation establishments at Lancing, Denstone and Hurstpierpoint.

The last thirty years of the nineteenth century produced significant developments both in the concept and provision of secondary education for girls. Only after considerable hesitation were girls' schools included in the investigations of the Taunton Commission, and pioneers like Beale, Buss and Davies invited to give evidence. Only twelve endowed schools for girls had been found in the whole of England. By contrast in 1895 the Bryce Commission listed eighty such schools, and commented that 'there has probably been more change in the condition of the Secondary Education of girls than in any other department of education'. The change was reflected not only in the Commission's terms of reference and inquiries, but also in its composition, for it included three females in Lady Frederick Cavendish, Dr Sophie Bryant, Buss' successor at the North London Collegiate School, and Mrs E.M. Sidgwick, Principal of Newnham College Cambridge.

Thus by 1900 opportunities for girls in secondary education, where some notion of equality had been established, had outpaced those in other facets of society. Restrictions still continued in higher education. Oxford did not grant full degrees to women until 1920, Cambridge not until 1948. Not until 1928 did women acquire the vote on equal terms with men. Schoolteaching apart there were few openings for women in professional or other skilled forms of employment.

'Organise your secondary education'

In the last quarter of the nineteenth century the ideal of basic education for all, which had been a permanent feature of English history since the coming of Christianity, received a new formulation in terms of compulsory, age-specific, elementary school attendance. At this time, however, compulsory secondary schooling for all would have been considered quite inappropriate, not least by working-class parents and children (imagine the response to a proposal for compulsory university education today). Nevertheless the advent of compulsory elementary schooling did concentrate attention upon three historic issues — what was the second stage of education, how could it be better supplied, and who should have access to it?

In answer to the first question, by 1900 three points had been resolved. Schooling, rather than domestic education or apprenticeship had come to be the norm, and the boys' public school its most successful and prestigious form. Thirdly the principle of public secondary schooling for girls had been established.

More contentious, however, were the roles of scientific and technical education, higher grade schools and pupil-teacher centres. In some public schools science and engineering came to occupy an important place. For example in 1893 at Dulwich College, a reformed endowment which had expanded into a large public day school, 93 of the 600 boys were on the science and engineering sides, with a further 230 learning physics and 228 chemistry.[39] A new concept of second stage education, however, was being formed in institutions like the Liverpool School of Science. Classes first began in 1861 in the Free Library, and continued in a number of evening centres until a central building was acquired in 1901. Students were entered for the Department of Science examinations. In 1885 of 1,100 enrolled seven passes were achieved at honours level, 139 at advanced and 359 at elementary. Of 1,005 class entries in 1904, 155 were above the elementary standard.[40]

The position of higher grade schools was particularly ambiguous. These central schools which catered for older and abler elementary pupils came under school board aegis and were financed partly from the elementary education rate. School board officials, and those of the Education Department had therefore to maintain that they were essentially elementary schools. In fact some of the work was of advanced or 'secondary' standard, whilst its nature was determined largely by the need to seek grants from the Science and Art Department. In many areas higher grade schools contained pupils who might otherwise have attended grammar or private schools. In 1895 the President of the Association of Headmasters of Higher Grade Schools claimed that these schools were 'as much preparatory schools for the university colleges, especially their technical and scientific sides, as the grammar schools are for the older universities'.[41] A Board of Education minute of 1900, however, whilst acknowledging the principle of higher elementary schools, established an age limit of fifteen years, thus effectively preventing direct university entrance.

Pupil-teaching centres provided another upthrust from the elementary system. For example in 1903 the Leicester pupil-teacher centre had an enrolment of 350, including practising, unqualified teachers who attended evening and Saturday classes. By 1906 numbers had passed the 1,000 mark. These included, since the minimum age for becoming a pupil teacher had been raised to sixteen, 262 intending pupil teachers aged between fourteen and sixteen who attended full time in what was virtually a secondary school.[42]

In 1902 the new LEAs were given powers to co-ordinate different types of education and to provide both secondary schools and teacher training colleges. Now at last Matthew Arnold's oft repeated plea to 'organise your secondary education' could receive serious attention. New county secondary schools were established, based in some cases upon former higher elementary schools or pupil-teacher centres. The last pupil-teacher centre in London closed in 1911.[43] Some of the particular dimensions of the higher grade tradition were continued in new 'central' schools. These were popular with working-class parents and children, but later were to receive strong criticism from those who saw the central schools as an inadequate substitute for 'real' secondary schools. By 1914 there were fifty central schools in London, providing commercial and industrial courses for children who might stay on until fifteen or sixteen years of age.

At the turn of the century, however, there was a genuine and widespread fear that secondary education was taking too scientific, technical and vocational a turn. Science grants and whisky money were bidding fair to confine serious classical and literary studies to the public and elite grammar schools. In consequence regulations of 1904 required that secondary schools, in order to qualify for grants from the Board, must provide a general education, mental, moral and physical, for pupils up to and beyond the age of sixteen. Manual training was to be included for boys and housewifery for girls, but the rest of the core curriculum, apart from physical training, was to be of a broad academic nature. In 1904 the minimum time to be allotted to these subjects was — Science (both theoretical and practical) and Mathematics a total of seven and a half hours, English, History, Geography and a foreign language a total of eight hours. This was very different from the idealised classical curriculum of a boys' public school, but not unlike the reality of many second grade grammar schools of the last quarter of the nineteenth century. Latin indeed could be dispensed with altogether.[44] Board of Education statistics for 1912 show that of 885 secondary schools, 128 had no Latin. On the other hand 73 schools provided courses with a vocational bias, either rural, commercial, domestic or engineering.[45] In 1907 the minimum subject quota times were withdrawn. In 1911 the Board's *Annual Report* 'emphasized the need of departing to some extent from the academic bias of the traditional secondary school curriculum and of giving greater prominence to work of a practical and vocational character'.[46]

Pupils

In the years after 1902 numbers of pupils in grant-aided secondary schools in England and Wales rose rapidly, to total some 200,000 by 1914. In London, where there were many public and private schools, secondary places in 1904 were estimated at 11,000. By 1919 these had more than trebled to 36,000. Twenty-three county secondary schools provided for 8,072 pupils, including 5,419 girls.[47]

Between 1895 and 1906 the number of local authority scholarships in secondary schools increased from 2,500 to more than 23,000. In 1907 more than half the pupils in grant-aided secondary schools had previously attended elementary schools. Some half of these, nearly 24 per cent of the total, paid no fees. In October of that year, after an increased grant had been given to secondary schools willing to offer 25 per cent of their places as free places to pupils who had attended elementary schools for at least two years, the proportion rose to 27 per cent. In 1924 over two-thirds, in 1937 over three-quarters of children in grant-aided and maintained secondary schools were former elementary school pupils. By 1926 Bradford, Manchester, Salford and Sheffield had abolished all fees in maintained secondary schools.

The School Certificate and Higher Certificate examinations introduced in 1917 had the effect of standardising the secondary school curriculum and of confirming its academic nature. Though there were subsequent modifications, candidates for School Certificate had to satisfy examiners in each of the three areas: English subjects, foreign languages, science and mathematics. These examinations also gave a boost to the meritocratic ideal. Nearly half the scholarship pupils who left grammar schools in 1926-7 obtained the School Certificate, as compared with only 20 per cent of the feepayers.[48] Possession of the certificate became a general passport to safe employment at sixteen in a range of professional, administrative and clerical occupations. In 1925-6, at least 47.5 per cent of boys and 30.2 per cent of girls went directly from grammar schools to professional or clerical employment. A decade later the figures stood at 46.1 per cent and 43.9 per cent whilst a further 13 per cent of the boys and 28.4 per cent of the girls proceeded to some form of higher education.[49] Small wonder that some poor families, accustomed to the insecurity of employment in such industries as mining, textiles and shipbuilding, scrimped and saved to send and keep their children at grammar schools. Competition was fierce, with at times as many as twenty applicants per place. Those who reached matriculation standard, and qualified for university entrance, obtained the better jobs at sixteen or seventeen. For those who actually proceeded to university, success in the Higher School Certificate could lead to a subsidised place, and from 1920 to a state scholarship. In 1938 of 798 open scholarships at Oxford and Cambridge, 437 were won by pupils from grant-aided secondary schools, two-thirds of whom gained exemption from the payment of fees as a consequence of low parental income.[50]

Pupil numbers in secondary schools in England and Wales recognised by the Board of Education grew rapidly from the 188,000 of 1913 to the 363,000 of 1921, and then more steadily to reach 482,000 by 1936.[51] Some of this increase resulted from pupils staying longer at school. Indeed with the advent of the certificate examination grammar school pupils were required to stay at least until sixteen. This was one important factor in accounting for the large numbers of parents who in the inter-war years refused grammar school places on behalf of their children. Thus at Leicester the number of free places for elementary school children who qualified in the general examination rose from 150 in 1923 to

300 in 1939. Over the same period, however, the number of refusals rose from 84 to 215.[52] Detailed evidence of this phenomenon and of the general inequality of opportunity which deprived many children of the low paid from access to secondary schooling was supplied by Kenneth Lindsay. Lindsay, himself an ex-grammar school boy and holder of a fellowship at Toynbee Hall, later was to become parliamentary secretary at the Board of Education. His *Social Progress and Educational Waste: being a study of the 'free place' and scholarship system* (1926) showed that in Bradford, where secondary education was free, refusals exceeded acceptances, even amongst the first 200 qualifiers on the list. Lindsay concluded that the proved ability of at least forty per cent of the nation's children was being denied proper expression. The full extent of unproved ability had not yet been determined. In his judgement at least half of the pupils in elementary schools could profit by some form of post primary education up to the age of sixteen. Yet less than ten per cent of elementary school pupils proceeded to secondary schools and only twenty per cent of the nearly three million adolescents in England and Wales were in full time school attendance.

Adolescence

Concern for, and at times fear of, the adolescent, prompted a variety of solutions aimed at bridging the potentially 'dangerous' years between the end of elementary schooling and adult life. Some reformers sought to place, in opposition to street culture, indiscipline and petty crime, the ideals of service, order, responsibility and physical well being. The Boy Scouts, begun in 1907 with Baden-Powell's camp on Brownsea Island, claimed more than 100,000 members in the United Kingdom by 1910, the year in which the Girl Guides were founded. The inter-war years produced the National Association of Boys' Clubs, the Youth Hostels Association, and in 1935 the King George V Jubilee trust and appeal. Youth organisations with a more militaristic flavour, the Air Training Corps, the Army Cadets, the Girls Training Corps, reflected both the threat and the reality of a second world war. The McNair Committee[53] reported in 1944 on the supply, recruitment and training of youth leaders as well as teachers. In 1960 the Albemarle Committee[54] concluded that there was an urgent need for a trained force of youth leaders who in a period of rising affluence could guide the fourteen to twenty year olds by means of association, challenge and training. An emergency training centre was opened in Leicester, and a Youth Services Development Council established.

Further education

A second approach to the adolescent was to provide a combination of work and education, as in the scheme for compulsory day time continuation schooling to eighteen contained in the Education Bill of 1918. This measure, paradoxically, ended the existing half time system by removing all exemptions from the school leaving age of fourteen. Opposition, particularly from Lancashire MPs where there was still a high proportion of teenaged workers, led Fisher to postpone for seven years the operation of the act upon those over sixteen. Instead young people between fourteen and sixteen were required to attend school for 320 hours per year. In London, for example, plans were drawn up for this group to attend for a course of general education in two four-hour sessions per week, and for vocational courses to be provided from 1928 for the sixteen to eighteen year olds. Though several schools were established in London and other centres, only at Rugby did day continuation survive the slump, expenditure cuts, and the widespread opposition of employers, parents and prospective learners. A similar scheme for day continuation until eighteen in county colleges as contained in the 1944 Act failed to materialise.

In the last twenty years further education, as it has come to be known, has assumed a more important place in the public education service. In the 1950s a third of boys leaving school still proceeded to apprenticeships, though the term was used to cover a multitude of situations. In 1959 the Crowther Report[55] on the education of fifteen to eighteen year olds showed the weakness and relative inefficiency both of this form of training and of much of the part-time day and evening work which took place in technical and further education colleges. Only one candidate in eleven completed the full National Certificate course, only one in thirty within the designated period of time. Only eight per cent of girls, as opposed to a third of boys, received part time day release. A White Paper of 1962 confirmed these findings and concluded that the unco-ordinated decisions of a large number of employers were not the most effective means of planning for this form of education and training. As a result the Ministry of Labour was empowered to set up industrial training boards and a Central Advisory Council was established. The most recent developments in this area have been not merely to provide for the continuing education and training of those in employment, but also for those school leavers for whom there are no jobs. Technical colleges and colleges of further education provide a variety of courses, full time, sandwich, day release and evening, and attract both adolescent and adult students.

Secondary schooling for all

A third approach emerged in *The Education of the Adolescent* (1926), the report of the Hadow Committee whose membership included R.H. Tawney,[56] author of *Secondary Education for All: a policy for Labour* (1922). Though its terms of reference specifically excluded existing secondary schools, the Committee's report proposed that the 'tide which begins to rise in the veins of youth at the age of eleven or twelve' necessitated a new form of universal school provision. This new concept of 'post primary' or secondary education for all was, however, nowhere properly defined. It was to take place in a variety of schools — grammar, junior technical, selective central, non-selective central henceforth to be known as 'modern' — and in senior classes in all age schools.

Throughout English history the second stage of education had been essentially a means of preparing a specific group of young persons, selected by birth, patronage or ability, for the particularly important social and economic roles which they would be likely to assume in adult life. This third solution to the problem of adolescence which emerged in the first half of the twentieth century was based upon six broadly held principles or assumptions. These were: firstly, that secondary education for all could be achieved through secondary schooling for all. Secondly that this would require an extension of the period of age-specific schooling initially to fifteen and subsequently to sixteen. Thirdly that it would be necessary to provide different types of school according to the different abilities of children and in anticipation of their future adult roles. Fourthly that some form of identification and selection would be necessary and that a reasonably accurate system could be devised. Fifthly that the existing network of schools could be adapted over a period of time to produce such a system, and that it would not be necessary to start anew. Finally it was assumed that the public and other private schools would continue to be largely independent of the state organised system.

These beliefs underlay the Hadow Report of 1926, the Spens

Report[57] of 1938, the Norwood Report[58] of 1943 and the 1944 Education Act. Thus Spens approved the existence of separate grammar, modern and technical schools, though recommending an increase in the numbers of the last. Spens' proposals for parity of esteem, a common curriculum in the first two years of secondary schools with further opportunities for transfer at age thirteen, were to be repeated in the Norwood Report of 1943. Norwood, who had himself been the headmaster of Harrow before becoming president of St John's College, Oxford, provided in his report the classic statement of the tripartite system. The three types of secondary schools, it was asserted, corresponded to three types of human being. These were the grammar school child 'interested in learning for its own sake', the technical school child 'whose interests and abilities lie markedly in the field of applied science or applied art' and the secondary modern child who 'deals more easily with concrete things than with ideas'.

The 1944 Act gave official recognition to the three successive stages of primary, secondary and further education, and raised the school leaving age to fifteen, though this was not implemented until 1947. Since no particular mention was made of types of secondary schools in most parts of the country the tripartite division continued.

Post-war criticism of universal schooling as a means of providing secondary education for all centred around three main issues. The most important and the most neglected was focused upon aims and curricula, and proceeded from the consumers themselves. In 1966 an inquiry[59] conducted into the attitudes of young school leavers showed that these pupils and their parents saw the most important purpose of schooling as being preparation for employment. Secondary school teachers, however, had little experience of the jobs to which some pupils would proceed and scant opportunity of preparing them for external examinations. In the same list of twenty-four objectives, therefore, head teachers of these schools assigned examination achievement and 'things of direct use in jobs' to the lowest two places. Little wonder that the secondary modern school struggled hard to find an identity! Introduction of GCE and CSE examinations, principally in academic subjects, whilst giving some greater unity of purpose, could only confirm its second or third rate status.

A second criticism concerned the selection process. The view that basic intelligence could be identified and measured with sufficient accuracy to justify assigning children at eleven years to one of the three types of school came under increasing attack. Research showed that scores on intelligence quotient (IQ) tests could be improved by coaching, even by as much as by sixteen points in one hour. The third anxiety concerned the relationship between social class and academic achievement. In 1956 it was calculated that the mean IQ of children of the highest occupational groups was greater by fifteen or twenty points than that of the lowest.[60] A survey in the early 1960s of over 1,000 public school boys who had failed the 11 plus examination showed that about 70 per cent achieved five or more passes at O-level.[61] Conversely in 1954 an official report on early leaving found that whereas in a sample group, given equal distribution, some 927 children of unskilled workers should have been in grammar schools, the actual number was only 436. Even more disturbing was the poor performance of these pupils in academic terms. 284 or roughly two thirds, failed to pass three O-levels.[62] In the 1960s explanations of such phenomena centred around home influence, expectations and socio-linguistic codes. By the 1970s more attention was being paid to secondary school curricula, particularly in the context of theories concerning the sociology of knowledge.[63] Recruitment of an all-graduate teaching force, however, has re-emphasised the links between the curricula of higher education and secondary schools.

Comprehensive schools

Comprehensive secondary schools which would take all children from the surrounding area were seen by many as the answer to these three problems. Their supporters predicted broader curriculum choice, an end to selection, and the promotion of social harmony — liberty, equality, fraternity, no less. Opponents expressed concern for academic standards, pointed to the inequalities inherent in neighbourhood schools, and deplored the impersonal nature of mammoth-sized institutions. Whilst the debate raged with assertions other counter assertions on both sides some authorities experimented with multilateral and comprehensive schools. Reform began in the Irish Sea. The Isle of Man reorganised in 1947; Anglesey County Council announced the abolition of its selection examination in 1952. The first purpose-built comprehensive in London, Kidbrooke, an all-girls 13-form entry, was opened in 1954. In 1965 LEAs were requested to submit reorganisation plans in accordance with the Labour government's determination 'to end selection at eleven-plus and to eliminate separatism in secondary education'. In

1972 the school leaving age was raised to sixteen. By 1980 when over eighty per cent of secondary age pupils were in comprehensive schools a new ideal and a reality of secondary education for all had been created.

Independent schools

Separatism of another kind, however, continued in primary and secondary education. Twentieth-century private progressive schools included Summerhill, founded in 1924 at Lyme Regis by A.S. Neill and moved to Suffolk three years later, Dartington Hall in Devon in 1926 the creation of the Elmhirsts, and Beacon Hill in Sussex in 1927, the brainchild of the Russells. New public schools in the nineteenth-century mould were few in number though Stowe (1923) and Gordonstoun (1934) were soon to make their mark. Suggestions for closer co-operation between independent and maintained sectors as contained in the reports of the Fleming Committee[64] of 1944 and the Newsom Commission[65] of 1968, however, produced little result. Indeed one link was broken. Since 1919 some grammar schools had received direct grants from the Board of Education. This system continued under the 1944 Act. Direct grant schools were required to provide a minimum of twenty-five per cent free places for children from local authority primary schools. Other fees were graduated according to parental income. From 1974 attempts to integrate these schools into the comprehensive system led to the majority of the 178 direct grant schools moving into the independent sector.

Though in the 1930s many independent schools were in dire financial straits, state secondary education for all as implemented in the post war era has not yet curbed the popularity of the public schools, nor the continued predominance of their ex-pupils in many high places. Threats, or promises, of outright abolition by Labour politicians not having been implemented, their immediate future would appear to be governed, as in the past, by social, economic and educational rather than political factors.

Conclusion

In the last twenty years many previously widely-held beliefs about secondary schools have been reversed. Selection on grounds of ability for different types of school has been discredited. Existing schools, some of high status and centuries old, have been abolished. A new ideal has arisen — that of the common school. Two of the other six principles outlined on pages 119–20 — compulsory school attendance to sixteen, and the continuation of the independent sector — have so far remained unchanged. Now that secondary school reorganisation has virtually been completed, the most fundamental issue can be approached anew. To what extent can genuine second stage education for all be provided in a school context?

NOTES

1 **Orme** (1976), p. 201.
2 **Moran** (1979), p. 7.
3 **Leach** (1911), p. 401.
4 Hair on the crown of the head was shaved or clipped as a sign of dedication to the special service of God.
5 **Leach** (1911), p. 401.
6 **Leach** (1911), p. 413.
7 **In recognition** of the three major Christian festivals, and of the most important event in the agricultural calender. Leach (1911), p. 339.
8 **Leach** (1911), p. 343. The wording of this comment (c.1385) by John Trevisa has been modernised.
9 **Orme** (1973), p. 89.
10 **Simon** (1966), p. 344.
11 **Dissenting academies** are considered in Chapter 6.
12 **Simon** (1966), p. 15.
13 Several examples are given in N. Hans, *New Trends in Education in the Eighteenth Century* (1951), pp. 63–115.
14 **Cressy** (1975), pp. 108–9.
15 **Cressy** (1975), pp. 109–10.
16 **J. Lawson,** *Medieval Education and the Reformation* (1967), pp. 71–2.
17 **Cressy** (1975), pp. 8, 10.
18 **A contentious subject.** *See* for example D. Cressy, 'School and College Admission Ages in Seventeenth-Century England', *History of Education* (1979), 8(3), and its reference to earlier articles in the same journal by Demolen, Charlton and Stone.
19 **Cressy** (1975), p. 97.
20 *See* **L. Stone,** 'The Educational Revolution in England 1560–1640', *Past and Present* (1964), 28.
21 **W.K. Jordan,** *Philanthropy in England 1480–1660* (1959) remains the standard work; M. Feingold, 'Jordan Revisited: Patterns of Charitable

Giving in Sixteenth and Seventeenth Century England', *History of Education* (1979), 8(4), its most recent critic.

22 **Cressy** (1975), p. 24.

23 **Cressy** (1975), p. 19.

24 *See* A.M. d I. Oakeshott, 'The Restoration and the Grammar Schools', *Journal of Educational Administration and History* (1973), 5(2), p. 2., W.A.L. Vincent, *The Grammar Schools* (1969), pp. 6–7.

25 **J. Simon,** 'Private Classical Schools in Eighteenth-Century England: a Critique of Hans', *History of Education* (1979), 8 (3).

26 **M.V. Wallbank,** 'Eighteenth-Century Public Schools and the Education of the Governing Elite', *History of Education* (1979), 8(1).

27 Quoted in J. Lawson, *A Town Grammar School through Six Centuries* (1963), p. 171.

28 **A.A. Mumford,** *The Manchester Grammar School 1515–1915* (1919), p. 193.

29 **D. Robson,** *Some Aspects of Education in Cheshire in the Eighteenth Century* (1966), pp. 44–65.

30 **J.R. de S. Honey,** *Tom Brown's Universe* (1977), p. 273.

31 **Maclure** (1979), pp. 87–8.

32 **B. Simon,** *The Two Nations and the Educational Structure 1780–1870* (1974), p. 320. P.P. 1867–8, xxviii, *Report of the Royal Commissioners on Schools not comprised within Her Majesty's two recent Commissions on Popular Education and Public Schools.*

33 There is a useful summary in P. Gordon, *Selection for Secondary Education* (1980), pp. 114–17.

34 P.P. 1895, xliii–xlix, *Report of the Royal Commission on Secondary Education.*

35 **J. Kamm,** *How Different from Us. A Biography of Miss Buss and Miss Beale* (1958), p. 116.

36 Quoted in Kamm (1958), p. 73.

37 Quoted in M.C. Borer, *Willingly to School. A History of Women's Education* (1976), p. 279.

38 **S. Fletcher,** *Feminists and Bureaucrats* (1980), p. 151.

39 **R.J. Palmer,** 'The Influence of F.W. Sanderson on the Development of Science and Engineering at Dulwich College, 1885–92', *History of Education* (1977), 6(2), p. 130.

40 **G.W. Roderick** and M.D. Stephens, *Scientific and Technical Education in Nineteenth-Century England* (1972), pp. 49–61.

41 **O. Banks,** *Parity and Prestige in English Secondary Education* (1955), p. 24.

42 **Seaborne** (1967), pp. 51–2.

43 **Maclure** *One Hundred Years of London Education 1870–1970* (1970), p. 92.

44 Though 'the Board will require to be satisfied that the omission of Latin is for the advantage of the school'.

45 **Banks** (1955), p. 75.

46 **Banks** (1955), pp. 72–3.

47 **Maclure** (1970), p. 88.

48 **M. Hyndman,** *Schools and Schooling in England and Wales. A Documentary History* (1978), p. 86.

49 **Banks** (1955), p. 170.

50 **Hyndman** (1978), p. 88. **Open** scholarships (which included 'exhibitions' generally of lesser value), were open to all persons of the right gender. **Closed** scholarships were usually restricted to pupils from a particular school.

51 **Seaborne** (1967), p. 62.

52 **Seaborne** (1967), p. 64.

53 Its main concerns, however, were the training, status and salaries of schoolteachers.

54 The first major report on the youth service.

55 **The Crowther Report** recommended full time education to eighteen for half the population by 1980 and compulsory part time education for the remainder.

56 **R.H. Tawney** (1880–1962), president of the Workers' Educational Association (WEA), 1928–44, whose academic career was spent at Oxford and the London School of Economics, where he was Reader and subsequently Professor of Economic History 1919–49.

57 **Report of the Consultative Committee** of the Board of Education on Secondary Education with Special Reference to Grammar Schools and Technical High Schools.

58 **Report of the Committee** of the Secondary Schools Examination Council on Curriculum and Examinations in Secondary Schools.

59 Published as *Schools Council Enquiry I* (1968). The Schools Council for the Curriculum and Examinations established in 1964 includes teacher, LEA and DES representatives.

60 **H. Silver** (ed.), *Equal Opportunity in Education* (1973), pp. 147–8.

61 **Hyndman** (1978), p. 154.

62 **Maclure** (1979), p. 237.

63 **In the sense** that secondary school curricula concentrated upon 'high status' knowledge which was irrelevant to the experience, interests and aspirations of large numbers of pupils.

64 **Report of the Committee** on Public Schools appointed by the President of the Board of Education.

65 **Report** of the Public Schools Commission.

6 Higher Education

Medieval Origins

Higher education has been interpreted in various ways; for example as the education of the upper ranks of society, as preparation for the elite professions, as the study of higher subjects and as the final stage in the process of formal schooling. The key institution around which the very concept of higher education in English history has been formed, was a product of the twelfth and thirteenth centuries.

From the Norman conquest until the fourteenth century French was the vernacular language of the aristocracy and of the court. Boys would be educated initially at home, and then usually in the household of another member of the nobility where they would acquire the military, management and social skills appropriate to their role in society. Girls too from this social group would be educated in a domestic environment or in a nunnery.

Prior to 1066 Benedictine monasteries probably constituted the most advanced centres of formal learning in England. After the Conquest, however, and particularly from the renaissance of the twelfth century, five major branches of medieval higher education can be identified.

The first were the cathedral schools, as at Exeter, Lincoln, Salisbury and York, which functioned as centres of higher education for the local clergy. By the thirteenth century formal lecture systems under the control of the chancellor were provided in the higher subjects of theology and law.

The four orders of friars, Dominicans, Franciscans, Carmelites, and Augustinians, also provided in their houses training in arts, philosophy and theology. There was no single centre and student friars moved around the appropriate houses both in England and on the Continent. A library catalogue of 1372 from the Augustinian friary at York lists 656 volumes containing over 2,100 treatises, including Euclid's ten books, and major Arabic and Jewish works.[1] In addition houses of study were established at the universities. The influence of the great Franciscan masters, Roger Bacon and

William of Ockham, was predominant in the Oxford schools of the thirteenth and fourteenth centuries.

The monastic orders similarly developed some of their own centres for higher learning in or near the university towns. At Oxford Rewley Abbey for the Cistercians and Gloucester College for the Benedictines were established in the 1280s. In 1435 St Mary's College was founded for the Augustinian canons.

The Universities of Oxford and Cambridge

The universities themselves constituted the fourth and most important development in medieval higher education. Whereas the greatest of medieval universities, that of Paris, originated from the cathedral school of Notre Dame, English universities developed not in the cities of Exeter, London, Salisbury or York, but in the towns of Oxford and Cambridge.

By the early thirteenth century both universities were recognisable if amorphous communities of masters and scholars. Students lodged where they could, in private houses or hostels, masters taught in churches or rented rooms and relied upon students' fees for their incomes. At Oxford friction between town and gown appears to have been common with frequent riots, brawls, disputes, dispersions and migrations. In 1209 some Oxford scholars, following a murder and the hanging of three of their number, departed to Reading. Others repaired to the schools at Cambridge which by 1231 was a recognised *studium generale*[2] with its own chancellor.

During the thirteenth century many students lived in halls, presided over by principals who were thus able to exercise some control over their scholars' academic and other pursuits. By the fifteenth century, when residence in halls or hostels had become compulsory, these institutions were in turn being supplanted by the colleges. Colleges were not confined to Oxford and Cambridge. For example in 1262 Bishop Bridport founded a college for a warden, two chaplains and twenty fellows at Salisbury, a city to which some Oxford scholars had repaired after the dispersion of 1238. Known subsequently as De Vaux, a name probably derived from one of the Paris colleges, it lasted until 1542, and is further evidence of the study of the liberal arts and theology at Salisbury in the thirteenth century.

University colleges were usually small, endowed, self-governing bodies of fellows, comprising a few elite graduate scholars who were thus enabled to undertake the lengthy and arduous studies required for the master of arts degree, and degrees in the higher faculties of law, medicine and theology. Merton College was the first to be formally constituted at Oxford in 1264, with preference given to kinsmen of the founder, Walter of Merton, former chancellor of Henry III. The warden and two ministers of the altar were originally to live on the manor of Maldon near Merton in Surrey, the proceeds of which were to support twenty scholars 'living in the schools at Oxford, or elsewhere where a University may happen to flourish'.[3] The scholars were to live together in an inn and to wear similar clothes as a mark of their union. Subsequently the whole enterprise was located at Oxford in a house adjoining St John's church. Peterhouse, the first Cambridge college, dates from 1284 and supported fourteen fellows.

Colleges were usually endowed by prelates or other wealthy benefactors, and had strong personal or regional connections. For example in 1314 Walter Stapledon, bishop of Exeter, founded Exeter College at Oxford for thirteen scholars from the counties of Devon and Cornwall.[4] Scholarships were available for undergraduates of two years' standing to support them for up to thirteen years whilst they studied for the higher degrees.

The most important university college of the first half of the fourteenth century was King's Hall,[5] Cambridge, which dates originally from 1317, and was endowed with a permanent home by Edward III some twenty years later. King's Hall was supported from exchequer revenues by eleven successive English kings from Edward II onwards, until in 1546 it was incorporated into Henry VIII's new foundation of Trinity College. Its original purpose was to prepare scholars nominated by the crown from amongst the boys of the Chapel Royal for further service in church and state. King's Hall remained under direct royal control and patronage throughout the medieval period, unlike King's College, Cambridge, founded in 1441 by Henry VI where from the beginning power was granted to the provost and fellows. King's Hall was exceptional for its royal connections and size, and provided some forty per cent of all Cambridge college fellowships in the fourteenth century, as did Merton at Oxford prior to 1379. It was also the first college of either university regularly to admit undergraduates. By 1350 King's Hall comprised both undergraduates and graduate fellows. In the next one hundred years some half of the second degrees taken by senior members of the college were in civil law.

The foundation of New College, Oxford, in 1379 by William of

Wykeham marked three further stages in collegiate development. Firstly it established a definite relationship between school and college inasmuch as boys would proceed thither from Winchester, its separate but complementary grammar school. Secondly provision was made both for undergraduates and senior members, and for the formal instruction of the former by the latter by means of a salaried tutorial system. Thirdly both in buildings and numbers New College was much greater than any previous collegiate foundation. It boasted a warden and seventy fellows, together with chaplains and choristers. Its purpose-built structure included chapel, hall, chambers and library around an enclosed quadrangle with cloisters to the west and kitchens to the east.

In the fifteenth and sixteenth centuries the colleges which had been intended principally for a minority of privileged and senior scholars, began to recruit fee-paying undergraduates as well. At the same time much of the teaching passed from the control of the regent masters into the hands of the college tutors. The first college lecturership was probably established at God's House, Cambridge in 1439, the college founded for the specific purpose of providing grammar school masters. Of more general significance were the lecturerships in philosophy and theology instituted at Magdalen College, Oxford in 1479. Their teaching was to be open without fee to all members of the university. By the second half of the sixteenth century, in spite of royal attempts to revitalise university lecturing, teaching, residence and discipline were largely under college control.

From the thirteenth century the arts course was the basic staple of university studies with higher faculties of theology, civil law, canon law and medicine. The full arts course to master's level took seven years in itself. A first degree in divinity required a further seven years of study with two more for the doctorate, and only slightly less rigorous requirements in the other higher faculties. Small wonder that a majority of medieval students probably departed the university without any degree, and that by the fifteenth century dispensations from the full statutory requirements of duration of studies were being sought, and granted. Though new degrees were instituted, in grammar in the fourteenth century and in music in the fifteenth, there were few students in these subjects or in medicine. By the fifteenth century, though theology still occupied the pride of place, 'queen of the sciences', a study of law was being seen as the chief pathway to success in church and state. From the thirteenth to the fifteenth centuries Oxford, which had a long-established reputation as a centre for the study of grammar, also became known for the instruction given in practical subjects. Though business administration, accounts, conveyancing, writing and similar subjects were not accorded degree status their study came under the control of the university authorities.[6]

The arts course was based generally upon the seven liberal arts and in particular upon logic and the three Aristotelian philosophies, metaphysical, moral and natural. All teaching and study was in Latin. After four years of diligent attendance at lectures in which the master expounded the prescribed texts and various glosses upon them, and successfully engaging in various repetitions, questionings and responsions — a system of continuous oral assessment — the student would be awarded bachelor status. Three years of further study led to the degree of master of arts. Now for two years he had the duty of lecturing himself. He also became a member of Convocation, the body which determined the university's statutes and chose the chancellor.

Students came to the university from the age of fourteen. There were no females amongst them. Though virtually all social ranks appear to have been represented the 'middling' group probably predominated. Many fell into debt and either withdrew, took on the duties of servants, or had recourse to borrowing from one of the various university chests of money bequeathed for this purpose by wealthy benefactors. Younger students relied upon parental or other family support, patronage or scholarships. Study in the higher faculties was often only made possible by the securing of a benefice with the dispensation of absence for several years for the purpose of study.

To be a university scholar could be a life in itself. For example Chaucer's poor 'Clerk of Oxenford' put books and learning above temporal considerations — food, clothes, a good horse, property and wealth. Yet even those students who left without any degree would, as a result of their studies, the more easily secure posts as parish priests or schoolmasters. For those who completed the full course there was access to some of the highest posts in the land, as bishops, deans, chancellors, ambassadors and the like.

The Inns of Court

A fifth development of medieval higher education took place in London. Studies at the universities were conducted entirely in Latin, the appropriate language for the more universal, theoretical and scholastic dimensions of canon and civil law. Proceedings in the common law courts of the land, however, which were concerned with disputes arising from the practical, everyday problems of existence, were conducted in French or English. At the apex of this system were the King's courts at Westminster, whose lawyers during term time lived together in inns situated midway between Westminster and the City of London. The four Inns of Court — Gray's, Lincoln's, Inner Temple and Middle Temple, and the ten Chancery inns, became centres of legal training as well as of residence. Training was rigorous and practically based, often subsequent to a period of more academic study at one of the universities. Though the inns were originally simply organised along typical gild lines in respect to entry, training and qualification, they came to provide a basis not only for the first great secular profession in English history, but also assumed a wider role in the provision of higher education.

Three factors contributed to this development. The first was expense. Maintenance particularly at the Inns of Court, was costly, so that to become a judge, sergeant at law, or even an 'utter' or junior barrister grew beyond the reach of all but the most wealthy or well-supported. Secondly, from the fourteenth century the nobility and gentry had a legal duty to fulfil in their capacities as local, unpaid, justices of the peace. Finally some training in the common law was seen as a useful preparation for an office of state.

Sir John Fortescue, himself Chief Justice from 1442 to 1461, described the system in a treatise *De Laudibus Legum Angliae*, written about 1470.

> Hence it comes about that there is scarcely a man learned in the laws to be found in the realm, who is not noble or sprung of noble lineage ... In these greater inns, indeed, and also in the lesser, there is, besides a school of law, a kind of academy of all the manners that the nobles learn ... knights, barons, and also other magnates, and the nobles of the realm place their sons in these inns, although they do not desire them to be trained in the science of the laws, nor to live by its practice, but only by their patrimonies.[7]

Thus by the end of the medieval period the Inns of Court also provided institutionalised instruction in manners and exercises similar to that given in a noble or royal household. They fulfilled the dual function of professional training for the law, and general higher education for some of the sons though not the daughters of the wealthy and influential.

Conclusion

By the beginning of the sixteenth century the map of English higher education was very different from what it had been some five hundred years before. The monasteries had long since been eclipsed as the main centres of learning, and would soon disappear altogether. The education of sons of the nobility, the highest social class, was less concerned with military and more with civil skills. Indeed in youth the future scholars, bishops, judges, statesmen, knights, lords, even princes of the realm, might now meet in one single institution of higher education — the university. The university was a unique creation of later medieval western Europe, and Oxford and Cambridge its two classic and enduring English examples. The description *studium generale*, applied to these institutions from the thirteenth century, indicated a place of higher learning attracting scholars from a wide area. The term *universitas*, current from the fifteenth century, originally a general term for a group of persons with a common purpose and independent legal status and privileges, would henceforth particularly be associated with an academic institution.

The new ideals of the scholar and of academic freedom were forged by the masters and students of thirteenth and fourteenth-century Oxford and Cambridge as a result of diligent and unremitting application amidst poverty, disputes and migrations. The qualities of rigorous intellectual training and academic discipline commanded both general respect and the accordance of specific rights and privileges. The universities undertook the greatest intellectual task of the time, the reconciliation of the learning of classical antiquity with the fundamental tenets of the Christian faith. The opinions of their leading scholars were eagerly sought in the great theological, political and social questions of the day. They provided a new location for the professional training of those who would occupy some of the highest places in church, households and state. They were a means of some social mobility, a pathway whereby the poor but assiduous scholar might attain intellectual eminence, wealth or high office. By the sixteenth century, however, in common with the Inns of Court, Oxford and Cambridge were also becoming finishing schools for the sons of the noblest families in the land. Their particular combination of social and intellectual pre-eminence was to have a profound effect upon the evolution of English higher education and of English society.

Sixteenth to Eighteenth Centuries

Oxford and Cambridge in transition

In the one hundred years following the 1530s the universities underwent further substantial changes.

Some of these were a continuation of trends already current in the fifteenth century, others were a direct consequence of the English Reformation. Thus the opinions of both universities were sought on the legality of Henry VIII's marriage to his deceased brother's widow, and on the issue of papal jurisdiction. As a result of the dissolution of the monasteries with the consequent loss of many important libraries the university houses of monks and friars were also closed. Many of the buildings, however, were subsequently incorporated into new college foundations, for example Magdalene at Cambridge and Trinity at Oxford. The year 1546 saw the new formulations of Christ Church, Oxford and Trinity College, Cambridge, and the endowment of five Regius professorships at Oxford in Greek, Hebrew, civil law, divinity and physic, to complement those founded at Cambridge some six years before.

In the years 1535–59 royal determination to secure religious orthodoxy led to a series of visitations and expulsions. By the early seventeenth century a formula requiring subscription to royal supremacy, the thirty-nine articles and the Book of Common Prayer was established which was to last until the nineteenth century. Puritanism flourished in some of the Cambridge colleges, however, and Emmanuel in 1584 and Sidney Sussex in 1596 were founded for the express purpose of providing preaching ministers. In 1571 Jesus College, Oxford was founded by Hugh Price specifically for Welshmen.

Both universities, or rather their colleges, continued to grow in numbers, reaching a peak in the 1630s in excess of 4,000 students, possibly a higher proportion of the total population than at any time until the twentieth century. In 1621, 784 students matriculated at Oxford, a total not to be equalled again until 1883.[8] College powers increased apace. By the end of the sixteenth century no one could be admitted to the university except through a college, whilst teaching rested largely in the hands of college tutors. Though the democratic convocations of the medieval period continued in name, in reality power in both universities passed to an oligarchy of college heads and a vice-chancellor nominated annually from amongst their number.

Social distinctions within the colleges became more marked. Poor scholars continued in large numbers, many working their way by acting as servants to wealthier undergraduates, or by performing other menial duties within the college. But the trend most frequently remarked upon by contemporaries was the increasing number of noblemen or gentlemen commoners, many of whom had no intention of taking a degree, and who by payment of extra fees secured such privileges as dining at high table and exemption from the wearing of academic dress. Similarly in the Inns of Court there was a further increase in numbers of students not intending to follow the legal profession as such.

This influx of gentlemen's sons may be seen from two perspectives. Firstly in accordance with the humanist ideal it reflected the desire of the established and aspiring groups in society to acquire genuine literary and social skills in a college setting. Much value, for example, has been set upon the university education of the members of the Elizabethan and early Stuart House of Commons.

Sixty-seven of the 420 members of the House of Commons of 1563 are known to have been at Oxford or Cambridge. In the parliament of 1584 the number had risen to 145 and in 1593 to 161. Just over half the MPs in the parliaments of the first half of the seventeenth century were university educated. A hundred years later the proportion had fallen to forty-five per cent.[9] On the other hand many gentlemen commoners failed even to matriculate, let alone to take a degree. The exact nature and value of their university education is therefore difficult to determine. The former pattern of university teaching was in serious decline. The quality and curricula of college tutoring are a matter of some dispute, though there were individual examples of dedicated tutors and of rigorous studies in such subjects as Greek and Hebrew, mathematics and science. The situation was further complicated by the possibility from the sixteenth century onwards of reading for learning and for a degree in a way which had been impossible when books were in short supply. The higher faculties failed to develop. Theology and civil law were in decline, canon law was abolished altogether in 1535. Medical studies were still based largely on the works of Hippocrates and Galen.[10] Higher degrees, including that of MA, became more of a formality. The influences of Aristotle and scholasticism still predominated, and formal degree exercises until the nineteenth century were based on a now obsolete medieval practice.

The new social dimensions and increased numbers in the universities were reflected in the clergy of the Anglican church. Clerical dynasticism could now flourish openly. By the early seventeenth century, although the wealth and power of the episcopacy were in relative decline, a higher proportion of parish clergy were graduates and of some social standing. For example in 1580 in Worcestershire fewer than one quarter of the clergy were graduates. By the 1640s some eighty-four per cent had degrees.[11] The church indeed became a recognised career for younger sons of the gentry, deprived by the growing customs of primogeniture and entail of any hope of a landed inheritance.

Household and Grand Tour

Household and family education also flourished amongst the well-to-do during the sixteenth and early seventeenth centuries. Popular instruction manuals, included Castiglione's, *The Courtier* (1528), translated into English in 1561, and Elyot's, *The Boke named the Governour* (1531). The household of Sir Thomas More provided a prime example of the educative family, and one in which scholarship was as meet for girls as for boys. Some parents with less learning and inclination to assume such responsibilities employed a private tutor instead. It was the tutor's particular duty to accompany the eldest son on his foreign travels. The general aim of these journeys, which were a substitute for the pilgrimages and military campaigns of the medieval period, was to gain practical knowledge and experience of a wider world. Italy, the source of Renaissance and humanist learning was the particular goal. The Grand Tour, as it came to be known, was an expensive and distinctive conclusion of the higher education of the favoured sons of the upper ranks of society.

Seventeenth-century reformers, Gresham College and the Royal Society

Schemes to establish further centres of higher education, nascent colleges or universities outside the confines of Oxford and Cambridge, met with as much opposition in the sixteenth and seventeenth centuries as in the medieval period. Concern for the particular educational deficiencies of the North was reflected in three schemes in the years 1590–1604 for a university at Ripon, and at Manchester and York in the 1640s. The college established at

Durham in 1657 with Cromwell's support was not allowed to grant degrees, and naturally disappeared in 1660 with the Restoration. Similarly the more grandiose vision of Comenius and Hartlib for a government-supported college of pansophia, or universal wisdom, like Francis Bacon's scheme for Salomon's House, 'a series of laboratories devoted to every conceivable subject of experimental research',[12] came to nothing.

Bacon's aim was to base knowledge upon experimentation and experience. He sought to separate secular from religious learning. Salomon's House would have included observatories, underground laboratories, engines, furnaces, dissection rooms, experimental gardens and the like. Bacon deplored those who sought merely to expound and interpret the existing fund of knowledge, particularly when simply confined to approbation of 'the philosopher' — Aristotle.

John Milton was less critical than Bacon. He sought to reform rather than to replace. Latin, Greek, Hebrew, philosophy, literature both secular and divine, were still to be essential studies. He planned, however, to give more attention to modern languages, mathematics, scientific and practical subjects, including architecture, navigation and trigonometry. Milton's pamphlet *Of Education* published in 1644 envisaged the setting up of general academies fulfilling the roles of school and university in every major city.

William Dell, a graduate of Emmanuel who became master of Caius, in a pamphlet of 1649 entitled *The Right Reformation of Learning, Schools and Universities according to the State of the Gospel,* also sought to break the monopoly of Oxford and Cambridge. Dell's particular emphasis was the ideal of a priesthood of all believers. He objected to the control exercised by universities over the religious mentality of the country. The idea that true religion must be buttressed by ancient, monopolistic, academic foundation was anathema to many puritans. Dell argued for state supported universities:

> It would be more advantageous to the good of all the people, to have universities or colleges, one at least at every great town in the nation, as in London, York, Essex, Bristol, Exeter, Norwich and the like; and for the State to allow to these Colleges competent maintenance for some godly and learned men to teach.[13]

For other seventeenth-century radicals the simplest solution to the university problem as they saw it was the destruction of Oxford and Cambridge. Levellers like William Walwyn emphasized the virtues of honest, plain, ministers of the word, the true successors of Christ's apostles. With the Bible, preaching and teaching in English, there was no need for a priestcraft centred around the esoteric languages of Greek, Latin and Hebrew. Gerrard Winstanley, in a pamphlet of 1649 entitled *The New Law of Righteousness*, concluded that: 'the Universities are the standing ponds of stinking waters, that make those trees grow, the curse of ignorance, confusion and *bondage* spreads from hence all the nations over'.[14]

Nevertheless, even though Oxford had been the centre of the King's cause during the civil war, the universities survived the period of the interregnum essentially intact. They did not go the way of the King nor of the House of Lords, for Oliver Cromwell, himself a product of Sidney Sussex College, Cambridge, was, like Henry VIII a century before him, both socially conservative and an admirer of genuine learning. Rather than abolish Oxford he became its chancellor.

The greatest need, however, and the most frequently canvassed, was for a university in London, one which would draw upon the wealth of the city, reflect its concerns in commercial, scientific and technical subjects, and become a means of training for a wide group of occupations. There was a recent precedent in the Scottish capital. In 1582 James VI had granted a charter to the new university of Edinburgh, in spite of opposition from the existing universities of Aberdeen, Glasgow and St Andrews. In 1609 as King of England James laid the foundation stone of Chelsea College, intended as a protestant bulwark against the Roman Catholic faith. The college did not prosper, and in parliamentary discussions of 1641 Chelsea was considered as one of three possible sites for the location of Hartlib's pansophic college. By 1647 Hartlib himself was pinning his hopes on a thorough reform of another London institution of higher education, Gresham College.

Unfortunately the college established from 1596 as the result of the will of Sir Thomas Gresham which might have acted as the centre for such a university, was beset from the beginning by two major problems. The first was the will itself, particularly as confirmed by Act of Parliament in 1581, which rendered further amendment impossible, except by statute. The second was the intrusion of royal patronage into the appointment of professors. Thus the trustees had little chance of removing inefficient or absentee members of staff.

The first seven appointees were all Oxford or Cambridge men. Divinity, civil law, rhetoric, music, physics, geometry and astronomy were their subjects. The trustees, through their ordinances, encouraged lecturing in English. The Lectures in law, geometry and physic were to be related to practical issues, whilst the astronomer was to teach geography, navigation, 'and the use of the astrolabe and staff, and other common instruments for the capacity of mariners'.[15] In the first three decades of the seventeenth century professors of the calibre of Henry Briggs, Edmund Gunter and Henry Gellibrand made important contributions to the development of logarithms and of navigational instruments. Men such as these, were, as the trustees intended, available for consultation by scholars, gentlemen, merchants, sailors, boat builders, tradesmen, artisans and others. Mathematicians, surveyors, mariners, and instrument makers acknowledged their debts to the lectures and consultations held at Gresham College.

By 1635, however, a decline had set in, though in 1647 Hartlib, and in 1649 William Petty, himself subsequently a professor of the college as was Christopher Wren, produced radical schemes for reform. These envisaged a purely scientific institution with further professors of magnetism, optics and technology. Nothing came of these proposals, indeed Petty himself as an absentee professor of music set a poor example. From 1666 following the Great Fire the college buildings were taken over by the City Corporation, and later became the home of the Royal Society.

The Royal Society was but the most famous of a number of groups which sought to promote a more scientific and experimental approach to knowledge and higher education. It originated in part from a group of mathematicians, scientists and physicians who in the 1640s met in London both in private houses and at Gresham College. When in 1648 one of their number John Wilkins, Cromwell's brother in law, became warden of Wadham College the focus shifted to Oxford. In 1659, when Wilkins became master of Trinity, Cambridge, interest returned to London where two of the Wadham dons, Lawrence Rooke and Christopher Wren were now professors at Gresham. Late in 1660 the group, though declining to found a college for the promotion of 'Physico-Mathematicall Experimentall Learning', agreed regularly to meet, debate and discuss such concerns. In 1662 the Royal Society was formally incorporated with the blessing of Charles II.

Though the society faced many early problems, principally opposition from the universities and a shortage of funds, it soon boasted a library, various scientific collections, numerous publications including the *Philosophical Transactions* and some of the greatest minds of the age. Robert Boyle and Christopher Wren had been members of the founding group, Evelyn and Pepys lent their aid, John Locke was elected a fellow in 1668 whilst Isaac Newton[16] became president.

Oxford and Cambridge in decline

Religious conformity had been required of the universities since the medieval period. The Act of Uniformity of 1662 which prescribed political and religious allegiance to the restored king and Anglican church was a natural and in some ways moderate response to the preceding years of puritan rebellion, civil war and republic. By the later 1660s the universities appeared to be flourishing and numbers of entrants rose to a peak of about 850.

At Cambridge the first Lucasian professor of Mathematics, Isaac Barrow, virtual inventor of differential calculus, was succeeded in 1669 by Newton. His work on the theory of gravity, and the *Principia Mathematica* published in 1687, established the place of mathematics within the university arts course, and began the Cambridge tradition of excellence in this field. At the same time Oxford scholars were engaged in a new kind of literary and historical research. In 1689 George Hickes produced the first Anglo-Saxon grammar, and Edmund Gibson's text of the Anglo-Saxon Chronicle was published in 1692. Queen's College became the centre of Anglo-Saxon study under Edward Thwaites, elected fellow in 1698 and preceptor in Anglo-Saxon and professor of Greek until his death in 1711.

Both universities continued to produce able and influential scholars throughout the eighteenth century. Oxford, which though numerically stronger than Cambridge, has been subjected to harsher criticism, could boast Henry Aldrich, dean of Christ Church, the noted logician, architect and musician, the astronomer Halley, Kennicott in Hebrew, Blackstone in law, and John Wesley,[17] elected to a fellowship at Lincoln College in 1725.

By the 1680s, however, admissions to both Oxford and Cambridge were in decline, a decline which reached its nadir in the 1750s and 1760s. This may be accounted for in part by the continued exclusion of protestant nonconformist and Roman Catholic sections of the community. It reflected also the failure of the universities to become places of education for professions other than the church. At the same time opportunities for social advancement through the church had diminished. The more lucrative livings had become the preserves of the younger sons of the established classes. Though there were notable exceptions, including Newton, the likely fate of many a poor sizar or servitor (as the young undergraduate who worked his way through college was called), was to become a poor curate or chaplain. Younger sons of the gentry who sought to make their way in the world in non-clerical professions, army, navy, commerce, East India Company and the like, had less reason to spend time at university where costs were high. Their status as gentlemen was already assured. Their concern was to find the means of support appropriate to it.

Though in the Middle Ages students had at times been attracted to universities by the fame of particular scholars, instruction was generally of a formal nature by means of lecture. From the sixteenth century collegiate instruction provided a new and distinctive element in English higher education, the provision of a tutorial system within an institutional context. Undergraduates would have rooms on the same staircase as their tutor, or nearby. The tutor would be responsible for the mental, physical and spiritual well-being of his charges. He would also supervise their manners, morals and finances and generally stand *in loco parentis*.

From the   sixteenth and seventeenth centuries come several examples of conscientious, devout and learned tutors who exercised a profound influence over their students. These bachelor dons would provide individually-tailored reading lists, give daily lectures, tutorials and work assignments, begin and end each day with prayers, and be present with students in hall and chapel. In the sixteenth century many tutors probably contented themselves with some four or five students. Some, however, like John Preston at Queens' admitted sixteen fellow-commoners in one year alone.

The tutorial system became a permanent feature of Oxford and Cambridge. John Wesley as an undergraduate at Christ Church was in the charge of the conscientious Henry Sherman and George Wigan. Wesley's own career as tutor at Lincoln from 1729 was characteristically thorough. His eleven pupils attended him daily for academic study, and on Sundays for religious instruction. He also accompanied some of them outside the university on various excursions. Though Wesley can hardly be taken as a typical tutor, even Edward Gibbon's much-quoted autobiographical strictures on his fourteen months at Oxford from 1752–3, contain some grudging approval of his first tutor at Magdalen, Dr Waldegrave. Gibbon admitted him to be 'a learned and pious man, of a mild disposition, strict morals, and abstemious life'. It was the fifteen year-old Gibbon who withdrew from the daily tutorials which Waldegrave began with him, yet he still preferred his tutor's company to that of other students, 'and in our evening walks to the top of Headington Hill, we freely conversed on a variety of subjects'.[18]

Such favourable recollections of the tutorial relationship should be set against other frequently condemned (or envied) features of eighteenth-century university life. There were indolent, pleasure-seeking dons and students, as in every age. Colleges could become closed oligarchies from which younger fellows looked for a means of escape via a college living or preferment to the joys of rural bliss and holy wedlock. The dining hall and postprandial port acquired for many a greater significance than the college chapel and celebration of the sacraments. Conversation might centre around national and college politics, sport, scandal and personal anecdotes, rather than on major academic and theological issues.

John Wesley gave full vent to his disapproval of these practices in what, not unnaturally, proved to be his last university sermon, delivered in 1744:

> Is this city a Christian city? Is Christianity, scriptural Christianity, found here? ... Are you lively portraitures of Him whom ye are appointed to represent among men? ... Is this the general character of Fellows of Colleges? I fear it is not. Rather have not pride and haughtiness of Spirit, impatience and peevishness, sloth and indolence, gluttony and sensuality, and even a proverbial uselessness, been objected to us, perhaps not always by our enemies, not wholly without ground.[19]

Godly learning, preservation of knowledge, and the training of the intellect were traditional aims of universities which persisted into the seventeenth and eighteenth centuries. Aristotelianism continued to dominate the arts course, particularly at Oxford where the anti-metaphysical doctrines of Ramus had gained little hold. Standard texts prescribed by statute in the sixteenth century — Aristotle, Plato, Virgil, Horace, Cicero, Euclid,[20] Hippocrates, Galen and the like — were basically those studied in the medieval period. The seventeenth century witnessed a similar combination of scholastic philosophy and classics within the university curriculum. Logic, ethics, physics, metaphysics, mathematics, grammar and rhetoric were the subjects of study. Declamations, given in English in the early years of the course and in Latin in the final year, were opportunities for students to show their proficiency in classical knowledge and style in a set piece. Disputations were required proofs of the mastery of logic, metaphysics and rhetoric. Jeremy

Bentham, in his later years a stern critic of the University of Oxford, as a thirteen year-old undergraduate at Queen's in 1761 wrote to his father:

> I have sent you a declamation I spoke last Saturday with the approbation of my acquaintances ... I have disputed too in Hall once and am going to again tomorrow. There also I came off with honour, having fairly beat off, not only my proper antagonist with arguments, the invalidity of which I clearly demonstrated ... Indeed I am very sorry it did not come to my turn to dispute every disputation day: for my own part, I desire no better sport.[21]

Academies and the New Learning

John Locke emerged as the chief critic of the Oxford curriculum in the later seventeenth century. He advocated a minimum of classical authors, a general toleration in matters religious and academic, and declared that Bacon and Descartes were of more use than Aristotle in promoting rationality and logical thinking. Student notebooks from the late seventeenth and early eighteenth centuries show that whilst the traditional authors were still recommended, many tutors were prescribing a much wider range of reading, study and even experimentation, including the works of Bacon, Boyle, Descartes, Hobbes,[22] Newton and Locke himself.

Locke's writings found a truer spiritual home in the dissenting academies which came into being as a result of the conformity legislation of the 1660s. Their first tutors were the ejected Puritan dons and ministers, for example Thomas Cole, Locke's former tutor at Christ Church established an academy at Nettlebed in Oxfordshire in 1666. Their original purpose was the professional training of ministers, and higher education of laymen, whose denominational principles henceforth would exclude them from the English universities. Nonconformist academies, however, were neither large nor particularly numerous. Until the 1690s they were private, even clandestine affairs, usually with but one tutor instructing a small group of students in his own house.

The academies of the eighteenth century were of a more public nature. Of the two most famous Northampton was established in a town equidistant from Oxford and Cambridge and with a medieval tradition as a seat of higher learning. Philip Doddridge its first tutor was a product of the very broad education provided by John Jennings at Kibworth Academy in Leicestershire. Lectures at Northampton were given between 10 a.m. and 2 p.m., and the first two years devoted largely to subjects of the *trivium* and *quadrivium*. Some language coaching was provided in the evenings.

Northampton Academy Time-table.[23]

a.m.		p.m.	
6.	Rise	2.	Dinner.
6.10.	Roll-call and prayers. Private reading.	7.	Evening prayers. 'Tutorials' or "coaching" in languages.
8.	Family Prayer. Breakfast.	before 9.	Supper
		10.	Gate locked.
10–2	Lectures.	10.30.	Students in their own rooms.

Lectures from 10 a.m.—2 p.m.

First year	Second year	Third year	Fourth year
Logic	Trigonometry	Natural ⎱ History	Civil Law
Rhetoric	Conic Sections	Civil ⎰	Mythology
Geography	Celestial	Anatomy	and Hiero-
Metaphysics	Mechanics	Jewish	glyphics
Geometry	Natural and	Antiquities	English Hist.
Algebra	Experimental	Divinity	Hist. of Non-
	Philosophy	Orations	conformity
	Divinity		Divinity
	Orations		Preaching
			Pastoral Care, etc.

Doddridge began with but three students. His original intention was to provide a course for intending ministers only. Though lay students were subsequently also admitted, numbers rarely exceeded fifty at any one time, and totalled not more than 200 before 1751. Sixty per cent were trained for the ministry.

Warrington Academy opened in 1757, and in a life of little more than a quarter of a century educated 393 students. Though the courses taken by 197 of these are not specified, of the remainder 98 were entered for Commerce, 52 for Divinity, 24 for Medicine and 22 for Law.[24] Warrington was presided over for nineteen years by John Aikin, a former student and tutor of Northampton, who held a DD of Aberdeen. Joseph Priestley, himself educated in the early 1750s at Daventry to which Northampton Academy had removed after Doddridge's death, was tutor in languages and *belles lettres* from 1761-7. In his *Essay on a Course of Liberal Education for Civil and Active Life* (1765), Priestley argued that 'different and better furniture of mind is requisite to be brought into the business of life'. Priestley himself taught Latin, Greek, French and Italian at Warrington, and encouraged the development of courses in history, geography, chemistry and anatomy.

The dissenting academies have frequently been praised for their committed tutors, enlightened curricula and teaching methods, moderate fees and high moral tone. Both in their own day, and subsequently, they were favourably compared with contemporary Oxford and Cambridge. On the other hand, even the academies of the eighteenth century were often small, migratory and short lived. They failed to emerge either as permanent centres of higher education, or as major training grounds for a variety of occupations.

The eighteenth century witnessed further schemes for promoting higher education in London. Daniel Defoe had undertaken a broad range of studies at Newington Green Academy under Charles Morton, himself a former student of Wadham during the Wilkins era. Neither Defoe's project for a University of London as outlined in his *Augusta Triumphans* (1728), however, nor the new centres of higher education established in the capital in 1742 and 1745 met with success.

Nevertheless science and the arts flourished through clubs, societies and private patronage. One such was the Society for the Encouragement of Arts, Manufactures and Commerce in Great Britain, established in 1754 by a group which included Henry Baker, Defoe's son in law. The British Museum, on the other hand, was a public institution and made London the home of the world's greatest library. It originated from a parliamentary response to the Sloane bequest of 1753. To this were added the Cotton and Harley collections, whilst in 1757 George II donated the 10,000 volumes and nearly 2,000 manuscripts of the royal library begun by Henry VII. Montague House, Bloomsbury, was purchased to house the collection which henceforth grew rapidly, both as a result of further bequests and in consequence of the Museum's right to a free copy within one month of publication of every new book printed in the United Kingdom.

The Royal Academy was founded in 1768 to promote taste and training in the visual arts, the Royal Institution in 1799 for the purpose of applying scientific knowledge to arts, manufacture and daily life. Though the Royal Institution originally provided a variety of lectures and lecturers, Landseer on art and Coleridge on poetry, its fame was to rest upon scientific experimentation. In

1801 Humphry Davy became director of the chemical laboratory, in 1812 Michael Faraday was appointed as his assistant.

Scientific and other new learning outside the capital drew upon the resources and personnel of dissenting academies, newly founded hospitals, local industry and peripatetic lecturers. In the second half of the eighteenth century scientific (philosophical) and literary societies flourished in many provincial towns, characterised by regular dinners, lectures, libraries, and even on occasion, publications. Erasmus Darwin, founder of the Lunar Society of Birmingham, so called because it met when the moon was full (though they dined at 2 p.m.), was a noted physician and scientist who had been educated at Cambridge and Edinburgh. His work on evolution anticipated that of Lamarck, and even that of his own grandson, Charles Darwin. Other members of the Lunar Society included Matthew Boulton, Joseph Priestley, James Watt and Josiah Wedgwood. The Manchester Literary and Philosophical Society, formed in 1781, developed an international reputation, and prompted the founding of similar societies elsewhere, including one in Newcastle in 1793. Manchester's first president was Thomas Percival, one of the first three students at Warrington Academy, its most famous member Robert Owen, then in Manchester *en route* from Montgomeryshire to New Lanark.

Law and medicine

In the second half of the sixteenth century the Inns of Court reached a pinnacle of prestige in higher education, aided by the patronage of such as William Cecil and Nicholas Bacon. One notable feature was the influx of Welshmen; for example eighty-nine were admitted at Lincoln's Inn in the years 1570–1610. There were new buildings — the hall of the Middle Temple was completed in 1570 — and the attendance of a galaxy of talented young men, including Philip Sidney, Francis Walsingham and John Whitgift at Gray's Inn alone.[25] Of the 420 members of the House of Commons in the Parliament of 1563, 108 had attended the Inns of Court. In 1584, 164 of the 460 members, and in 1593, 197 had been at the Inns, in each of these three instances a significantly higher number than had attended the universities.[26]

A hundred years later the Inns had declined in importance both as centres of general higher education, and as places of organised professional instruction. Henceforth intending barristers submitted rather to the gastronomic test of consuming a specified number of dinners in hall.

In the sixteenth century there was a renewed concern for the well-being of the body, as for the soul. Higher education of the medical profession was centred in London, and ultimately contributed to the foundation of the capital's university in the early nineteenth century.

Medical studies had flourished in the medieval Italian universities of Salerno and Padua. In the 1490s Thomas Linacre, having been awarded an MD at Padua, returned to England where he became attached to the royal household. Linacre's medical writings and influence with Henry VIII contributed to the incorporation of the Royal College of Physicians in 1518. The College attracted several eminent fellows including John Caius who in 1557 refounded Gonville and Caius College, Cambridge for the particular purpose of encouraging medical studies. In 1616 William Harvey who had studied medicine at Cambridge and Padua first announced to the world his theories concerning the circulation of the blood, in his capacity as lecturer at the Royal College of Physicians. Harvey, physician at St Bartholomew's Hospital, also attended the first two Stuart kings, and subsequently became warden of Merton College, Oxford.

Only the university educated, however, could secure the licence to practise of the Royal College, and in time this came to be further restricted to graduates of Oxford and Cambridge. In consequence by 1745 there were a mere fifty-two fellows, twenty-three licentiates and three candidates in the Royal College,[27] and the expansion of the medical profession was undertaken by two other groups, the surgeons and the apothecaries.

The Barber Surgeons Company was founded in 1540, a charter being granted by Henry VIII to its first president Thomas Vicary. This new body, with its hall, demonstrations and lectures, raised both the standards of surgery and the status of its practitioners. In the sixteenth century masters of the company were practising, practical men. Thomas Gale served with the armies of England and Spain, John Woodall also had military experience and became first surgeon to the East India Company. In less warlike times George Baker, master in 1597, became a member of the household of the choleric and much-travelled Earl of Oxford.

Seventeenth-century readers on anatomy to the Company included Richard Mead and William Wagstaff, who respectively advanced the reputations of St Thomas' and St Bartholomew's hospitals. In 1745 when the Barber Surgeons Company finally split into two, the new body of surgeons continued their teaching, examining and licensing functions in London and its surroundings. Further changes in 1800 and 1843 produced the Royal College of Surgeons.

Apothecaries were the third group of medical practitioners, members of the influential Company of Grocers. In 1617 the apothecaries were incorporated into a separate company, and soon acquired their own hall, library, gardens, botanising excursions and the power to regulate entry and apprenticeship. For many years apothecaries probably made the largest contribution to the treatment of the sick, and in an important judgement of 1703 the House of Lords ruled that apothecaries were indeed entitled to prescribe as well as to dispense medicines. Though there was considerable rivalry between the three groups, in 1773 John Lettsom formed the Medical Society of London, with a council comprising equal numbers of physicians, surgeons and apothecaries.

Many of the great London teaching hospitals were founded in the first half of the eighteenth century, including the Westminster (1719), Guy's (1725), St George's (1733) and the London (1740). Together with a number of private medical schools, including those of the noted brothers John and William Hunter, they confirmed the position of the capital as the centre of higher medical education in England and Wales. In 1834 in the early days of London University, 347 of the 469 students at Gower Street and 241 of the 446 at King's College were medical students.[28]

Nineteenth and Twentieth centuries

Oxford and Cambridge

In the first half of the nineteenth century the two ancient universities were as socially exclusive as at any other time in their long history. Students from humble backgrounds were virtually excluded, and more than half of Cambridge graduates and nearly two thirds of those from Oxford entered the church. Classics at Oxford and mathematics with subsidiary classics at Cambridge, remained the staple subjects, both justified in terms of rigorous intellectual training and liberal education. Some important changes occurred, the introduction of honours degrees and written papers, and by 1850 examinations in such subjects as natural sciences, law and history. Clubs and organised games flourished with intercollegiate and intervarsity contests — in particular the boat race and university cricket match.

Major grounds for criticism still existed. The restrictions on non-Anglicans, the doubtful intellectual quality of some college tutors, required to be both celibate and in holy orders, the continuing domination of the university by the colleges, the neglect of practical science and professional education, the exclusion of all but sons of the social elite, clergy, military, gentry and aristocracy, were matters of growing concern. In 1831 Sir William Hamilton declared in the pages of the *Edinburgh Review* that Oxford was no longer a public university 'but merely a collection of private schools'. In the pages of *Alton Locke* (1849) Charles Kingsley, though a former student and subsequently professor of modern history at Cambridge, drew attention to the privilege, wealth and hypocrisy which attended much of university education: 'And so these aristocrats of college dons go on rolling in riches and fellowships and scholarships that were bequeathed by the people's friends in old times just to educate poor scholars'.[29]

Significant changes occurred in the period 1850–1914. More students were recruited from the middling and lower levels of the middle class. Public, proprietary and reformed grammar schools provided a constant stream of applicants. In the 1850s dissenters were admitted to first degrees, from the 1870s they were eligible for fellowships. Dons no longer had to be celibate nor in holy orders. The curriculum was cautiously broadened. Law and history became separate subjects of study in the 1870s. In 1878 a board for the study of modern and medieval languages was instituted at Cambridge and the Oxford honours school in English was established in 1897. Cambridge forged ahead in its provisions for scientific subjects. In 1873 the Cavendish laboratory was opened where Clerk-Maxwell, Lord Rayleigh, J.J.Thomson and later Rutherford were to lead the world in experimental physics.[30] The mechanical sciences tripos was instituted in 1892.

The collegiate system, however, was not well adapted to the major expense and re-orientation necessitated by practical scientific study. In this period Oxford and Cambridge continued to provide an education which was liberal rather than professional, which aimed at thorough mastery of closely delimited existing areas of knowledge, principally in classics or mathematics, and which still put a premium upon teaching the old rather than researching the new. Such an education was justified as a supreme intellectual discipline, as an end in itself, as the means of producing a true gentleman, and as the best grounding for all honourable occupations, inasmuch as it was not a specific preparation for any single one. Oxbridge graduates, and some who failed to achieve a degree, continued to monopolise the top positions in politics, church, law, university, public school and administration both in the home civil service and in the empire. Of the 18 prime ministers 1815–1914 only three, Wellington, Russell and Disraeli, had not been educated at Oxford or Cambridge. Entry to the higher echelons of public service, even when opened to competitive examination, was still controlled by Oxbridge graduates who carefully tailored the new selection procedures to suit the education they had themselves experienced.

London and Durham

In the 1820s the recurring dream of a third English university, a university worthy of the nation's capital, took a new form in the shape of 'the cockney college', 'the godless institution of Gower Street'. It grew from the frustrations of radicals, dissenters and utilitarians with the social, religious and educational exclusiveness of Oxford and Cambridge. It drew rather upon examples of higher education in Scotland, Prussia and the USA. Many of its early supporters, Brougham, Birkbeck, Campbell, Hume, James Mill and Russell were Scotsmen or had been Scottish educated. University College London (as it was to be known from 1836) opened in 1828. There were no religious tests and no religious teaching. Immediately a rival college arose. At a meeting of June 1828 presided over by the Duke of Wellington and graced by an army of bishops and archbishops, the idea of King's College was born, to be incorporated by charter in the next year and opened in the Strand in 1831. In 1836 the University of London was established with powers not only to award degrees in various subjects, but also to affiliate other colleges throughout the country and grant degrees to their students. By 1851 some sixty medical and twenty-nine general colleges had been affiliated to the university. In 1858 University of London degrees were opened to all males, collegiate or non-collegiate (though not to females for another twenty years) who could pay the fees and pass the requisite examinations.

University College and King's College, though rivals, had much in common. They recruited students from a wider social range than did the older universities and sent them forth to a more diverse set of occupations. They provided broader curricula, including economics, engineering, law, classics, history, mathematics, modern languages and natural philosophy. Medical studies predominated in the early years, and physical science was also prominent, in spite of the considerable prestige of the Royal Institution and Faraday at this time. J.F. Daniell inventor of the hygrometer and of the improved electric battery was the first professor of chemistry at King's in 1831. Three years later Charles Wheatstone, pioneer of the electric telegraph, the dynamo and the 'bridge' was elected to the chair in physics.[31]

There was a common pattern of development. Each college had an associated proprietary school, a teaching hospital and gave assistance and support to a women's college — Queen's founded in 1848 and Bedford founded in 1849. Each experienced the same problems, problems to be shared with the other new university foundations of the nineteenth century — precarious finances and poor student numbers.

In the 1830s the great wealth of the chapter of Durham cathedral, its stalls worth on average some £3,000 a year, was apparently threatened by a reforming Whig ministry. Under Van Mildert, the last of the great palatine bishops, and his successor Maltby, a new university came into being. A draft scheme received parliamentary approval in 1832, in 1834 statutes were formulated and students admitted. A charter of incorporation giving the power to award degrees was secured in 1837. Yet in spite of cathedral patronage, the gift of Durham castle, the opening of residential halls in the 1840s and 1850s, and its unique position as the sole university of the north, by the middle of the century Durham had withered and almost died. In 1840 there were 82 students, 31 in arts, 30 in theology and 21 in engineering. In 1860 the total was only 51. Engineering had sadly declined with but one student. There were 30 in arts and 20 in theology. Evidence presented to the Durham University Commission of 1863 showed that the university had failed to establish a truly independent identity. Its image was that of a pale and largely unsuccessful imitation of Oxford and Cambridge. It was clerical, Anglican and exclusively male in character. The vast majority of its graduates, one witness suggested about nine tenths, proceeded to Anglican orders.[32]

Civic colleges

In the second half of the nineteenth century nascent university colleges were founded at Manchester (1851), Southampton (1862), Newcastle (1871), Leeds (1874), Bristol (1876), Sheffield (1879), Birmingham (1880), Nottingham (1881), Liverpool (1881), Reading (1892), and Exeter (1895). Welsh colleges included Lampeter (1822), Aberystwyth (1872), Cardiff (1883) and Bangor (1884). A charter for the University of Wales was granted in 1893.[33] Some were the creation of wealthy benefactors; John Owens at Manchester, H.R. Hartley at Southampton, Josiah Mason at Birmingham, Mark Firth at Sheffield. Others, as at Newcastle and Leeds, were launched by public subscription. The colleges at Bristol, Sheffield, Nottingham and Reading were much aided by the university extension movement. By the 1870s a syndicate for this purpose was established at Cambridge with as its secretary James Stuart, a Cambridge don who had pioneered the provision of public lectures to working-class audiences in the industrial midlands and north. This work was complemented from 1903 by the Workers' Educational Association.

Most civic colleges had strong industrial and scientific connections, connections reinforced from the 1870s by fears of a 'Great Depression'. They provided many leaders of the newer large scale industry, its managers and designers, its research staff and salesmen. The colleges themselves became major centres of industrial research, Leeds in textiles, Sheffield in steel, Birmingham in brewing, Liverpool and Newcastle in marine and London in electrical engineering. These, however, were not the only subjects of study. Owens College, Manchester for example, taught the humanities including classics and philosophy from its inception. Many students were part time and attended only in the evenings; the majority of these were engaged in non-degree work. For example of the 2,170 students at Sheffield in 1907–8 only one-third were day students, and only 139 were engaged in degree courses and three in postgraduate work. Though several colleges gained prestige by amalgamation with existing medical schools, they were still largely dependent upon London University examinations, and separate university status was only achieved with great difficulty.

In 1898 after a series of investigations, including two Royal Commissions, a University of London Act appointed commissioners whose statutes of 1900 transformed the university into a teaching institution with some twenty-four schools, including the two original colleges and the newly-created project of the Webbs, the London School of Economics. Other colleges aspired to, and soon achieved, the status of schools of the university.

In 1900 Birmingham achieved full university status, to be followed by Manchester and Liverpool in 1903, Leeds in 1904, Sheffield in 1905 and Bristol in 1909.

The new universities and university colleges of the nineteenth century transformed the concept of higher education. By the 1900s each major city had its university college. Such institutions were often important agencies of social mobility, particularly from 1902 when the new local education authorities were empowered to establish secondary schools and to give scholarships to university students.

The new universities also received growing support from central government funds. London University had received grants from the beginning, and in 1887 an annual sum of £2,000 was voted to the federal Victoria University of Manchester. From 1889 £15,000 p.a. was disbursed amongst the university colleges, eight years later it was increased to £25,000. On the eve of the First World War the sum had risen dramatically to some £170,000.[34] By 1938–9 nearly one-third, by 1951–2 nearly two-thirds of university income was derived from Treasury grants.

In the academic year 1913–14 there were 18,228 full time students in English universities and university colleges, together with a further 7,253 in Scotland and 1,230 in Wales. In 1800 the students at Oxford and Cambridge numbered 1,128, in 1913–14, 7,704.[35] Thus over this period whilst the population of England and Wales quadrupled that of the two older universities increased seven times, and the university population as a whole some seventeenfold.

The universities in the nineteenth century in maintaining or reasserting their predominant position in higher education underwent the most significant changes in their history. The extent of parliamentary and public concern is shown by the numerous commissions of inquiry which were set up, particularly into Oxford and Cambridge in the three decades before 1880 and into London in the three which followed.

The age old monopoly of Oxford and Cambridge, with all the restrictions which that had entailed, was finally broken. In the 1870s and 1880s women gained entry to the universities, though not necessarily on equal terms with men. Though the new English universities were not in general as democratic as those of Wales or Scotland they did provide an important means of upward social mobility. Some students from poorer homes were equipped with the necessary qualifications to move into professional, managerial and other occupations or status. They produced not only doctors, engineers and company directors, but also, for the first time in English history, the graduate schoolmistress. Universities became centres of research, including research into science and technology, the essential economic basis of industrialised society. They were thus by 1914 fulfilling a multiplicity of functions, both public and private. There can be few greater contrasts in English and Welsh educational history than that between the universities of 1914 and those of a century before.

The new professions

Similar changes were taking place in the extra-university world. Here too higher education was being redefined in terms of purposes, curricula and personnel.

The nineteenth century witnessed several answers to the question of higher education and training for the professions. This variety was nowhere greater than in the teaching profession itself. Formal apprenticeship and certification for elementary school teachers was introduced from 1846, but training colleges in the main (St Mark's was one notable exception) did not aspire to the provision of higher education. In 1870 about half of the certificated teachers in the country were women. By 1895 the proportion had risen to three-fifths, Maria Grey College for the training of women teachers was established in 1878, although acceptance of the general principle of training for teaching at the secondary level, as distinct from the possession of a degree, dates from the 1890s. Nearly a century later it is still not required for those who teach in higher education. No single professional body for teachers has emerged, in spite of repeated attempts to secure this, notably by the College of Preceptors, incorporated by royal charter in 1849.

On the other hand medical schools and medical training constituted an important element in the new universities of the nineteenth century, particularly in London. Control of the profession, principally by means of the maintenance of a register of qualified practitioners, was accorded to the General Medical Council, a body established in 1858 by Act of Parliament. The legal profession, on the other hand, declined the offer of a closer university connection. Examinations for solicitors were introduced in 1836 and made compulsory some seven years later. In 1846 a Select Committee on Legal Education reported the need for a rapid development of legal studies in existing universities, and for the creation of a new legal university, based on the Inns of Court. Ten years later a Royal Commission came to the same conclusion, but the opposition of Gray's and Lincoln's Inns proved to be insuperable.

Two colleges founded in the early nineteenth century by the East India Company, Addiscombe for soldiers and Haileybury for civilians, provided a genuine course of higher and professional education, including studies in oriental languages, sciences and the law. Sadly neither survived the reorganisation consequent upon the demise of the Company and the mutiny of 1857. Addiscombe was closed. Haileybury, sold in 1861, became yet another of the new breed of public schools. In 1871 the Royal Indian Engineering College was opened at Coopers Hill, near Egham in Surrey. Not all its students, however, proceeded to careers in India. Other bodies concerned with the professional training of engineers included the Institution of Civil Engineers founded in 1818, the Institution of Mechanical Engineers established at Birmingham in 1847, and the Society of Engineers based upon Putney College from 1854. In 1880 the Institution of Mechanical Engineers had 1,178 members. By 1900 this had increased to 5,583.[36]

Though engineering, for example, struggled to become an acceptable 'status' subject in early nineteenth-century higher education, the first chair at Oxford dates only from 1908. Important scientific societies were formed at this time: these included the Royal Astronomical Society (1820), the Zoological Society (1826), and the Royal Botanic Society (1839). The first meeting of the British Association for the Advancement of Science took place at York in 1831. Grants were made to assist scientific research and the foundation of local scientific studies encouraged.

The working classes

Many supporters of the major working-class movements of the first half of the nineteenth century were more interested in political economy and the price of bread, than in science and technology. Mutual Improvement Societies, Working Men's Associations and People's Colleges, Owenite and Chartist Halls grew up alongside Literary and Scientific Institutes and Methodist class meetings. Lectures, reading rooms, newspapers and periodicals, libraries and discussions provided a new educational context. Many of these institutions flourished but briefly and then disappeared. Others survived to become prestigious institutions of higher education. Thus the London Mechanics' Institution, established in 1823 at a great meeting of some 2,000 people, principally working men, with George Birkbeck in the chair, in 1920 became a part of London University as Birkbeck College.

In 1854 the London Working Men's College was founded by a group of Christian Socialists led by F.D. Maurice, professor of English literature and history and of theology at King's College London. In a building in Red Lion Square, recently vacated by the failure of the North London Needlewomen's Association, some 150 students were offered a wide curriculum ranging from algebra and arithmetic to politics and practical jurisprudence. Literary and artistic studies occupied a particular place, especially as taught by a galaxy of eminent Victorians including Burne Jones, Kingsley, Rossetti and Ruskin. Thomas Hughes, author of *Tom Brown's Schooldays* (1857), organised the boxing class and the volunteer corps. As a movement the working men's colleges were probably less successful than the mechanics' institutes, and towards the end of the century the curriculum of the London college was broadened to include commercial and technical subjects. Maurice and his helpers, however, who gave their services without fee, provided an important new dimension in the higher education of the working classes. They were supplying not merely the means of making better workers and better citizens, nor simple recreational pursuits, nor the indiscriminate dispensing of useful knowledge. Their aim was to bring working men into contact with the highest culture. Liberal education was provided in a liberal spirit.

The Extension movement, conceived by its founder James Stuart of Trinity College, Cambridge, as 'a sort of peripatetic university', was formally launched in 1873. A London Society for the Extension of University Teaching was constituted some three years later, and an Oxford delegacy in 1878. University extension was open to women as well as to men. Within two years the Cambridge syndicate was operating 100 courses with a total average attendance of over 10,000. By 1893–4 it was claimed that 60,000 students were attending extension courses. The great lecturers, like R.G. Moulton of Cambridge and G.W. Hudson Shaw of Oxford, could command vast audiences. For example over nine successive years Shaw's lectures at Oldham drew an average weekly audience of 650, with a final attendance of more than 1,000 in 1895.[37]

In 1890–1, of 457 courses arranged by Oxford, Cambridge and London, 191 were on natural science, 159 on history or political economy, 104 on literature, art or architecture, and three on philosophy. Courses were short — six to twelve lectures — but intensive, with printed syllabuses and lecture summaries, discussion periods, prescribed reading and written work. Examinations were held and certificates awarded. The work of the very best students was often favourably compared with that presented in final honours degree papers. Extension students came from a variety of backgrounds, though the charging of fees no doubt prevented the attendance of many members of the working classes. Daytime courses were attractive to the leisured groups in society, particularly women. Professional and businessmen, elementary school-teachers and artisans were prominent in evening courses.

In its numbers of students, admixture of social classes, opportunities for women, concept of liberal education for all, awakening of the older universities to their wider social responsibilities and contribution to the founding of the new university colleges, the university extension movement en-capsulated many of the most important developments in higher education in the modern period.

University extension and university consciences also produced the settlement movement. Samuel Barnett, vicar of St Jude's, Whitechapel, was the pioneer, aided by members of Oxford University, and Toynbee Hall, officially opened in 1885 as a social and educational centre, the prototype. On the other hand Ruskin College, originally founded in 1899 at Oxford as Ruskin Hall, sought rather to bring the working man to the university. Training in working-class leadership was provided with courses in eco-nomics, political science, public speaking and the like. From 1909 Ruskin came under the control of a council composed of representatives of various working-class bodies, including the TUC and the Co-operative Union. The WEA, originally 'An Association for promoting the Higher Education of Working Men' was established after a meeting held at Oxford in 1903. Its founder was Albert Mansbridge, a CWS clerk and lay preacher. By 1914 the WEA had 179 branches and 11,430 members, though the strength of the movement lay in quality rather than quantity. Tutorial classes were established in conjunction with the university extension movement. The first were at Rochdale in 1908 when 40 students pledged themselves to a three-year course in economic history under the guidance of R.H. Tawney. The WEA also established strong links with the revived adult schools which in 1909 reached a peak of more than 100,000 students.

Science and technology

Some mention has already been made of scientific and technical instruction in connection with the new universities of the nineteenth century. In the 1880s some of the old mechanics' institutes secured a new lease of life as centres of technical instruction. There were new foundations as well. Thus following a meeting of the City of London Livery Companies in 1876 the City and Guilds of London Institute for the Advancement of Technical Education was incorporated in 1880.Three years later the first English technical college was opened at Finsbury. Engineering, both mechanical and electrical, technical subjects, chemistry, applied art and trade classes were the areas of study. Within ten years the college had nearly 200 day and more than 1,000 evening students.

The Regent Street Polytechnic, reopened in 1882 by Quintin Hogg, a wealthy City merchant, achieved instant success. Within a year there were some 100 classes in a wide range of subjects, and 5,000 students. The City Parochial Charities Act of 1883 released a million pounds for this work, and with generous assistance from the City companies a further 13 London polytechnics were founded. Some like the Goldsmiths' Polytechnic at New Cross soon aspired to collegiate membership of London University. There was great variety in courses and levels of work, but by 1904, 500 polytechnic students were working for London degrees.

Ever since the Great Exhibition of 1851 there had been schemes to establish a technical university on the South Kensington site. In 1907 the Imperial College of Science and Technology was formed by an amalgamation of the Royal College of Science, the Royal School of Mines and the City and Guilds Central Technical College. Its promoters were Webb, Haldane and Rosebery, whilst financial support was secured from a variety of sources including Cecil Rhodes and the LCC. Imperial College started with 600 full-time students, and although separate university status was not achieved, it soon won an international reputation, meriting comparison with the Physical Technical Institute at Charlottenburg.

Wars and slump

In the years 1914–18 many thousands of young men, staff and students, departed their institutions of higher education never to return. War brought new urgency to the solution of old problems.

The Department of Scientific and Industrial Research was established in 1915. Many of its personnel and much of its work were to be university based. In the following year a committee, chaired by the physicist J.J. Thomson, was set up to investigate the role of science in education. Its report of 1918 emphasised the need for more postgraduate research in science and technology. After the war universities provided a new structure of research degrees at masters and doctorate levels. The University Grants Committee, which acquired permanent status in 1919, provided increased funds both for capital and recurrent expenditure. A system of 200 state scholarships was introduced in 1920, whilst other students received local authority grants. Some forty per cent of university students were receiving financial assistance from public funds by the later 1930s.

There was an immediate post-war boom. In the 1920s new university colleges were opened at Leicester, Exeter and Hull. Reading achieved full university status in 1926, remarkable both for its halls of residence and for its department of agriculture. The University of London underwent further reorganisation. In 1927 a central site was acquired in Bloomsbury, and the 'functional crag'[38] of the Senate House, erected thereupon. New statutes came into operation in 1929.

Amidst the economic depression and unemployment of the 1930s a period of retrenchment and re-examination ensued. Higher education was seen in terms of consumption rather than investment. Full-time university student numbers in this decade were static, or even in decline. There was a widespread feeling that the new universities had failed to make the grade, and that quality had been sacrificed to quantity. Critics from without, including the American Abraham Flexner, and from within, notably Ernest Barker, principal of King's College, London, called into question the standards, purposes and curricula of the university system of the 1930s. Flexner argued that domestic science, journalism, glass technology and similar courses were not proper subjects of university study. Barker warned against blurring the distinctions between universities and technical colleges and against the over-production of alienated intellectuals. Indeed in the later 1930s even schoolteachers, who constituted a significant proportion of graduates in the inter-war years, were in oversupply. In these circumstances it is not surprising that there were no new university foundations in the 1930s, and that even the 9,852 students of science and technology in the universities of 1922 had increased only marginally to 10,278 by 1938–9.[39]

Others, however, notably Lord Eustace Percy, President of the Board of Education, 1924–9, sought to develop from amongst the existing technical colleges genuine centres of excellence in higher technological study. A national system of awards was introduced with both government and professional backing. In 1921 the Board of Education and the Institution of Mechanical Engineers began a scheme of ordinary and higher certificates and diplomas in mechanical engineering. Certificates were for part-time, diplomas for full-time students. Other subjects to be added in the inter-war years included electrical engineering, chemistry, naval architecture and building. Technical education, however, remained an essentially part-time business. In 1938 for every full-time student in this area of further education there were some thirty part-timers.

During the Second World War the values of central planning and of scientific and technical excellence were clearly shown. Indeed for a few days in September 1940 the fate of the nation seemed to rest upon a handful of Spitfires and Hurricanes, and their pilots. With the first scent of victory there was a wave of idealism, a concern to establish a fairer society with the basis of a welfare state. Higher education was once more seen in terms of an investment in the future, but the way forward was far from clear. The Education Act of 1944 required local authorities to make provision for further education, but the county colleges never materialised. In the same year the McNair Report recommended the grouping of training colleges for teachers under university aegis in area training organisations.

In 1945 The Percy Committee on Higher Technological Education proposed the creation of Colleges of Technology, to provide courses of degree and postgraduate standards. After eleven years of fruitless debate a White Paper on Technical Education came to much the same conclusions. Accordingly in 1957 a new award, the Diploma of Technology was introduced and ten Colleges of Advanced Technology (CATs) established to teach it. Meanwhile the recommendations of the Barlow Committee on Scientific Manpower, whose report of 1946 had urged a virtual doubling of the output of university scientists and technologists, had been steadily implemented.

Robbins and expansion

The reports of the Robbins Committee on Higher Education of

1963 contained two major proposals. The first involved a further considerable expansion of numbers in higher education in Great Britain from 216,000 full-time places in 1962–3, to 560,000 in 1980–1. Such expansion it was calculated would involve an increase from eight to seventeen per cent in the proportion of the relevant age group for whom higher education would be provided, and a doubling from 0.8 to 1.6 per cent of the gross national product which would be devoted to this purpose.[40] The second proposal involved an increase in the proportion of the universities' share of entrants to higher education, from 55 per cent in 1962 to 60 per cent in 1980. Training colleges were redesignated as colleges of education and brought into closer relationship with university departments of education. A Bachelor of Education (BEd) degree was introduced. The ten CATs were simply transmuted into universities or university colleges, and the Dip. Tech. abolished. A Council for National Academic Awards (CNAA) was established in 1964 with the power to grant first and higher degrees to students in non-university institutions.

The Robbins projection of 390,000 students in higher education in Great Britain in 1973–4 had included some 51,000 on courses above GCE 'A' level standard in further education establishments. A White Paper of 1966 entitled *Plan for Polytechnics and other colleges* showed, however, that there were already more than 40,000 students engaged in such work in England and Wales alone. Thirty new centres of higher education in England and Wales were thus designated under the old title of polytechnics. By 1970 all but four were in operation. The new polytechnics provided a variety of courses, full and part time, for degrees, professional and other qualifications. Not all their work was of a scientific or technical nature. They have been called the 'comprehensive schools of higher education'.[41] The polytechnics like the further education colleges which expanded rapidly in this period, particularly in response to the Industrial Training Act of 1964,[42] remained under the control of local authorities.

Full-time university student numbers in Great Britain which by 1960 were at 100,000, double those of the pre-war era, had doubled again by the end of the decade. Former university colleges, including Nottingham (1948), Southampton (1952), Hull (1954), Exeter (1955) and Leicester (1957), achieved independent status. The University College of North Staffordshire, begun at Keele in 1950, achieved university status in 1962. Sussex, opened at Brighton in 1961, was the first of a new university breed, independent and degree-awarding from the start, and located on campus sites on the outskirts of rather smaller towns than hitherto. The example was quickly followed in the years 1963–5 by East Anglia (Norwich), Essex (Colchester), York, Lancaster, Kent (Canterbury) and Warwick (Coventry). There were variations in the pattern. A foundation year in arts and sciences was included in Keele's four year degree course. Sussex, which achieved an early popularity and prestige, was organised in schools of studies with multi-subject honours courses. York was based on the collegiate pattern. In the new foundations there seemed to be less of the old disciplines — classics, theology and law, even of science, and more of the social sciences — sociology, American studies and the like. Hard on their heels came the new technological universities. By 1967 eight of the ten CATs had achieved independent university status as Aston, Bath, Bradford, Brunel, City, Loughborough, Salford and Surrey.

During the later 1960s higher education evinced significant growing pains, and student protest came to a head in 1967–8. Universities, polytechnics, schools of art, even colleges of education were involved. There were international dimensions, against American involvement in Vietnam, and support for a new breed of folk heroes, Mao Tse-tung, Ho Chi Minh and Che Guevara. Generally speaking limited student representation on governing and academic bodies was secured, but attempts to transform institutions of higher education into thoroughly democratic bodies were unsuccessful.

The most radical new project of this exciting decade was outlined in a white paper of 1966 entitled *A University of the Air*. The Open University, as it was finally called, began in 1971 with 25,000 students. Courses were taught not merely by means of radio and television, but also included correspondence work, regular written assignments and tutorials, weekend and summer schools. The Open University, like the University Extension movement of a century before, drew adult students from all walks of life, including many non-graduate teachers, and many middle-class married (and unmarried) women.

Conclusion

Today it is argued, as in the 1930s, that the country cannot support the higher education system it has inherited. Determination to reduce the proportion of national wealth spent on this item has found expression in schemes to replace student grants with loans, and to curtail 'liberal' as opposed to 'useful' courses of study.

Yet recession, unemployment, underemployment and early retirement have led to an increase in the number of adults with the opportunity and motive for education. Age-specific compulsory schooling has redefined primary education in the nineteenth century and secondary education in the twentieth. Higher (in the sense of adult) education for all will surely be the major objective of the twenty-first century, though it will probably be neither compulsory, age-specific, nor school based. If a guaranteed education is the best means of allowing childhood to ripen in children and adolescence in adolescents, its capacity for promoting adulthood in adults must surely be tried. A new ideal of universal education beckons once more.

NOTES

1 **Moran** (1979), p. 27.
2 'A place of study open to people from all parts.'
3 **Leach** (1911), p. 171.
4 **Orme** (1976), p. 48.
5 **A.B. Cobban**, *The King's Hall* (1969).
6 **A.B. Cobban**, *The Medieval Universities* (1975), pp. 223–4.
7 **Sylvester** (1970), p. 77.
8 **V.H.H. Green**, *The Universities* (1969), p. 29.
9 **M.H. Curtis**, *Oxford and Cambridge in Transition, 1558–1642* (1959), pp. 268–9. Of the 635 MPs in the Parliament of 1974, 423 had been university educated.
10 **Hippocrates** (*c.* 460–377 BC), Greek physician, the traditional father of medicine. **Galen** (*c.*130–200 AD) physician to the Roman emperors.
11 **Green** (1969), p. 29.
12 **W.H.G. Armytage**, *Civic Universities* (1955), p. 95. **Francis Bacon** (1561–1626), philosopher, lawyer and precursor of inductive thought and scientific inquiry.
13 Quoted in Armytage (1955), p. 110.
14 Quoted in H. Kearney, *Scholars and Gentlemen* (1970), p. 111.
15 Quoted in I.R. Adamson, 'The Administration of Gresham College and its Fluctuating Fortunes as a Scientific Institution in the Seventeenth Century', *History of Education* (1980), 9(1), p. 17.

16 **Isaac Newton** (1642–1727), mathematician and scientist.
17 **John Wesley** (1703–91), the founder of Methodism.
18 **Sylvester** (1970), p. 215.
19 Quoted in V.H.H. Green, *A History of Oxford University* (1974), pp. 275–6.
20 **Euclid** (*c.* 300 BC) the Greek mathematician and father of geometry; the Roman poets **Virgil** (70–19 BC) and **Horace** (65–8 BC).
21 Quoted in Green (1974), p. 103.
22 **Robert Boyle** (1627–91), precursor of the modern sciences of chemistry and physics; **René Descartes** (1596–1650), French mathematician and philosopher, 'I think, therefore I am'; **Thomas Hobbes** (1588–1679), philosopher whose major work *The Leviathan* (1651) upheld the sovereignty of the state.
23 **I. Parker**, *Dissenting Academies in England* (1914), p. 86.
24 **Parker** (1914), p. 160.
25 **Armytage** (1955), p. 77, G. Williams, *Religion, Language, and Nationality in Wales* (1979), p. 177.
26 **K. Charlton**, *Education in Renaissance England* (1965), p. 137.
27 **Kearney** (1970), p. 145.
28 **Armytage** (1955), pp. 173–4. The foundation of the University of London is considered on pp. 149–50 of this chapter.
29 Quoted in Green (1969), p. 55.
30 **James Clerk-Maxwell** (1831–79), first Cavendish professor of experimental physics who translated the work of Faraday and others into a single mathematical theory, electro-magnetism; **John William Strutt,** 3rd Baron Rayleigh (1842–1919), mathematician, physicist and discoverer of argon; **Joseph John Thomson** (1856–1940), mathematician and physicist who worked in the fields of electrons and isotopes; **Ernest Rutherford** (1871–1937), physicist who split the atom and prepared the way for nuclear research.
31 **Armytage** (1955), p. 174.
32 **M. Sanderson** (ed.), *The Universities in the Nineteenth Century* (1975), p. 107.
33 **The present federation** of seven institutions also includes Swansea, the Welsh National School of Medicine at Cardiff and the University of Wales Institute of Science and Technology (UWIST).
34 **Sanderson** (1975), p. 188.
35 Figures taken from tables in Sanderson (1975), pp. 242–4.
36 **Roderick** and **Stephens** (1972), p. 16.
37 **T. Kelly**, *A History of Adult Education in Great Britain* (1962), p. 231.
38 **Armytage** (1955), p. 257.
39 **M. Argles**, *South Kensington to Robbins* (1964), p. 77.
40 **This was justified in terms of** 'economic growth and higher cultural standards'. Within twenty-four hours of the publication of the Report the Robbins targets until 1973 were accepted by the

government. The proportion of eighteen-year-olds entering higher education has levelled off at about thirteen per cent.

41 **H.C. Dent,** *1870–1970, Century of Growth in English Education* (1970), p. 160.

42 **By 1970,** under the provisions of this Act, twenty-nine boards had been set up to oversee the industrial training and education of some 16 million employees.

7 Conclusion

History may be defined as the study of the human past. It is firmly located in the dimension of time. Though historical study was once a private matter and is still undertaken by individuals, it is today a public discipline. Its purpose is to promote an enlarged understanding of the human condition; principally in the past, but also by inference in the present and the future.

Just as the concept of history has changed over time so has the meaning of the term education. For most of the period under consideration in this book it was principally defined in terms of religion, morals, vocation and social status. Schools were but one means of providing such education. Religious instruction naturally took a pride of place in any period in which the belief prevailed that ultimate destinies were controlled by a God, and that life on earth was but a brief prelude to another eternal existence.

Today it is widely assumed that the ultimate destinies of the nation (and of the world) are controlled by the human beings who inhabit it. Education in England and Wales is thus now more concerned with the values and rewards of this life than of an hereafter. It has a universal school base. Indeed the history of education over the last two hundred years has been interpreted as 'the rise of the schooled society'. Today its emphases are secular rather than religious, intellectual rather than moral, individual and competitive rather than societal and quiescent. The story, however, has no ending. Change (and the possibility of decay) are as real in the 1980s as at any time in human history.

In the future, determination to maintain a rising standard of living — perhaps the most widely shared ideal of our society — will doubtless produce further emphasis upon the investment notion of education and its scientific, technical and commercial dimensions. On the other hand shortage of employment — a seemingly inevitable consequence of such factors as changes in female education and expectation and the micro chip — must be rationalised into a shorter working day, week or life. Thus education both in its formal and informal senses having virtually monopolised the worlds of childhood and adolescence, may spread further into the adult years. For the first time in history higher education for all could become a reality, and strongly influence the development of new ideals both of the educated life and of the educative society. That such ideals are necessary in this nuclear age when the very future of this planet and of all life upon it rests immediately in the hands of the human race can hardly be doubted.

Select Bibliography

This bibliography provides a guide to the location of primary sources, journal articles and theses, together with lists of key secondary works.

Primary sources

The National Register of Archives, Quality Court, London, WC2 is the starting point for the location of unpublished primary material. The British Library, Great Russell Street, London, WC1 and the Public Record Office, Ruskin Avenue, Kew, Richmond, Surrey are the major national collections, complemented at the local level by County Record Offices and Public Libraries. The archive collections and libraries of academic institutions and educational societies constitute a further important source.

P. CUNNINGHAM, *Local History of Education in England and Wales: A Bibliography* (1976) University of Leeds, and W.B. STEPHENS, *Sources for English Local History* (1981) Cambridge University Press, are guides to local material.

C.W.J. HIGSON, *Sources for the History of Education* (1967, 1976) London: Library Association, is a list of historical material, including school books, contained in the libraries of institutes and schools of education and of some universities.

Copies of official publications on education may be found in a number of specialist libraries including that of the Department of Education and Science, Elizabeth House, York Road, London SEI.

Two guides published by the History of Education Society are M. ARGLES, *British Government Publications in Education during the Nineteenth Century* (1971) and J.E.VAUGHAN, *Board of Education Circulars: a finding list and index* (1972).

Journals

Three journals specialising in the subject are *History of Education* (1972 — in progress), *History of Education Society Bulletin* (1968 — in progress) and *Journal of Educational Administration and History* (1968 — in progress). The first two are journals of the History of Education Society, the third is published by the Museum of History of Education at the University of Leeds.

Other relevant articles may be found in a variety of journals. Of those devoted to education the *British Journal of Educational Studies* (1951 — in progress) has been the most important. There is a select list, compiled by D.W. Humphreys, of historical articles in the issues 1951–70 in *History of Education Society Bulletin* (1971) 7. The *British Education Index*, published quarterly, provides a complete and up to date list of all articles in educational journals.

Amongst historical journals *Past and Present* (1952 — in progress) has been particularly influential. There is an analysis of this contribution by J. Simon in *Oxford Review of Education* (1977) 3 (1).

Theses

V.F. GILBERT and C. HOLMES, *Theses and Dissertations on the History of Education presented at British and Irish Universities between 1900 and 1976* (1979) History of Education Society, and P.M. JACOBS, *History Theses 1901–70 Historical Research for higher degrees in the universities of the United Kingdom* (1976) Institute of Historical Research, University of London, are the basic guides. Both are kept up to date by regular supplements. See also the annual *Index to theses accepted for higher degrees by the universities of Great Britain and Ireland and the Council for National Academic Awards* London: Aslib.

Collections of documents

CRESSY, D. (1975) *Education in Tudor and Stuart England*. London: Arnold.

GOLDSTROM, J.M. (1972) *Education: Elementary Education 1780–1900*. Newton Abbot: David and Charles.

GOSDEN, P.H.J.H. (1969) *How They Were Taught. An Anthology of Contemporary Accounts of Learning and Teaching in England 1800–1950*. Oxford: Blackwell.

HYNDMAN, M. (1978) *Schools and Schooling in England and Wales: A Documentary History*. London: Harper and Row.

LEACH, A.F. (1911) *Educational Charters and Documents*. Cambridge: Cambridge University Press. (1971 reprint, New York: AMS Press).

MACLURE, J.S. (1979) *Educational Documents England and Wales 1816 to the present day*. London: Methuen.

SYLVESTER, D.W. (1970) *Educational Documents 800–1816*. London: Methuen.

General

ADAMSON, J.W. (1930) *English Education 1789–1902*. Cambridge: Cambridge University Press.

ARMYTAGE, W.H.G. (1964) *Four Hundred Years of English Education*. Cambridge: Cambridge University Press.

BARNARD, H.C. (1961) *A History of English Education from 1760*. London:

University of London Press Ltd.

BERNBAUM, G. (1967) *Social Change and the Schools 1918–44*. London: Routledge and Kegan Paul.

CHARLTON, K. (1965) *Education in Renaissance England*. London: Routledge and Kegan Paul.

COULTON, G.G. (1918) *Social Life in Britain from the Conquest to the Reformation*. Cambridge: Cambridge University Press.

CURTIS, S.J. (1967) *History of Education in Great Britain*. (7th edn) London: University Tutorial Press.

DENT, H.C. (1970) *1870–1970 Century of Growth in English Education*. London: Longman.

DOBBS, A.E. (1919) *Education and Social Movements 1700–1850*. London: Longmans Green (1969 reprint, New York: Kelley).

EVANS, L.W. (1971) *Education in Industrial Wales 1700–1900*. Cardiff: Avalon.

HANS, N. (1951) *New Trends in Education in the Eighteenth Century*. London: Routledge and Kegan Paul.

JARMAN, T.L. (1951) *Landmarks in the History of Education: English education as part of the European tradition*. London: Cresset.

JORDAN, W.K. (1959) *Philanthropy in England 1480–1660: a study of the changing pattern of English social aspirations*. London: Allen and Unwin.

LAWSON, J. (1967) *Medieval Education and the Reformation*. London: Routledge and Kegan Paul.

LAWSON, J. and SILVER, H. (1973) *A Social History of Education in England*. London: Methuen.

MIDWINTER, E. (1980) *Schools in Society. The evolution of English education*. London: Batsford.

OWEN, D. (1964) *English Philanthropy 1660–1960*. London: Oxford University Press.

RICHMOND, W.K. (1978) *Education in Britain since 1944: a personal retrospect*. London: Methuen.

SIMON, B. (1974) *The Two Nations and the Educational Structure 1780–1870*. London: Lawrence and Wishart.

SIMON, B. (1974) *Education and the Labour Movement 1870–1920*. London: Lawrence and Wishart.

SIMON, B. (1974) *The Politics of Educational Reform 1920–1940*. London: Lawrence and Wishart.

SIMON, J. (1966) *Education and Society in Tudor England*. London: Cambridge University Press.

WARDLE, D. (1974) *The Rise of the Schooled Society. The history of formal schooling in England*. London: Routledge and Kegan Paul.

WILLIAMS, J.L. and HUGHES, G.R. (eds) (1978) *The History of Education in Wales*. Swansea: Christopher Davies.

Local

BAMFORD, T.W. (1965) *The Evolution of Rural Education: Three Studies of the East Riding of Yorkshire*. Hull: Institute of Education.

COOK, T.G. (ed.) (1972) *Local Studies and the History of Education*. London:

History of Education Society, Methuen.

DAVIES, J.A. (1973) *Education in a Welsh rural county: 1870–1973*. Cardiff: University of Wales Press.

HISTORY OF EDUCATION SOCIETY, (1977) *Studies in the Local History of Education*. Occasional publication No. 3.

JOHNSON, M. (1970) *Derbyshire Village Schools in the Nineteenth Century*. Newton Abbot: David and Charles.

MACLURE, J.S. (1970) *One Hundred Years of London Education 1870–1970*. Harmondsworth: Penguin.

MALTBY, S.E. (1918) *Manchester and the Movement for National Elementary Education. 1800–1870*. Manchester: Manchester University Press.

MORAN, J.H. (1979) *Education and Learning in the City of York 1300–1560*. York: Borthwick Institute.

ORME, N. (1976) *Education in the West of England 1066–1548: Cornwall, Devon, Dorset, Gloucestershire, Somerset, Wiltshire*. Exeter: University of Exeter.

ROBSON, D. (1966) *Some Aspects of Education in Cheshire in the Eighteenth Century*. Manchester: Manchester University Press for Chetham Society.

RUBINSTEIN, D. (1969) *School Attendance in London 1870–1904: a social history*. Hull: University of Hull.

SEABORNE, M. (1967) *Recent Education from Local Sources*. London: Routledge and Kegan Paul.

SELLMAN, R.R.S. (1967) *Devon Village Schools in the Nineteenth Century*. Newton Abbot: David and Charles.

SIMON, B. (ed.) (1968) *Education in Leicestershire 1540–1940: a regional study*. Leicester: Leicester University Press.

STEPHENS, W.B. (1973) *Regional Variations in Education during the Industrial Revolution 1780–1870: the task of the local historian*. Leeds: University of Leeds.

VICTORIA COUNTY HISTORIES

WARDLE, D. (1971) *Education and Society in Nineteenth-Century Nottingham*. London: Cambridge University Press.

Chapter 1

ANDERSON, C.A. and BOWMAN, M.J. (eds) (1966) *Education and Economic Development*. London: Cass.

BLAUG, M. (1970) *An Introduction to the Economics of Education*. London: Allen Lane.

CLARKE, J., CRITCHER, C. and JOHNSON, R. (eds) (1979) *Working Class Culture: studies in history and theory*. London: Hutchinson with University of Birmingham.

DENT. K.S. (ed.) (1979) *Informal Agencies of Education*. History of Education Society.

DOUGLAS, J.W.B. (1964) *The Home and the School: a study of ability and attainment in the primary school*. London: MacGibbon and Kee.

GEERTZ, C. (ed.) (1963) *Old Societies and New States*. London: Collier-Macmillan; New York: Free Press of Glencoe.

HORN, P. (1978) *Education in Rural England 1800–1914*. Dublin: Gill and Macmillan.

LASLETT, P. (1965) *The world we have lost*. London: Methuen.

MATHIAS, P. (1969) *The First Industrial Nation: an economic history of Britain, 1700–1914*. London: Methuen.

MILLER, G.W. (1971) *Educational Opportunity and the Home*. London: Longman.

MITCHELL, B.R. and DEANE, P. (1962) *Abstract of British Historical Statistics*. Cambridge: Cambridge University Press.

MUSGRAVE, P.W. (ed.) (1970) *Sociology, History and Education*. London: Methuen.

MUSGROVE, F. (1966) *The Family, Education and Society*. London: Routledge and Kegan Paul.

PERKIN, H.J. (1969) *The Origins of Modern English Society 1780–1880*. London: Routledge and Kegan Paul.

REEDER, D.A. (ed.) (1977/8) *Urban Education in the Nineteenth Century*. London: Taylor and Francis; New York: St Martin's Press.

SMELSER, N.J. (1959) *Social Change in the Industrial Revolution: an application of theory to the Lancashire cotton industry, 1770–1840*. London: Routledge and Kegan Paul.

STENTON, D.M. (1957) *The Englishwoman in History*. London: Allen and Unwin; New York: Macmillan.

STONE, L. (1977) *The Family, Sex and Marriage in England 1500–1700*. London: Weidenfeld and Nicolson.

THOMPSON, E.P. (1963) *The Making of the English Working Class*. London: Gollancz.

WEST, E.G. (1975) *Education and the Industrial Revolution*. London: Batsford.

WRIGLEY, E.A. and SCHOFIELD, R.S. (1981) *The Population History of England 1541–1871*. London: Edward Arnold.

Chapter 2

ADAMSON, J.W. (1946) *The Illiterate Anglo Saxon and other essays on education, medieval and modern*. Cambridge: Cambridge University Press.

ALTICK, R.D. (1963) *The English Common Reader: a social history of the mass reading public, 1800–1900*. Chicago, London: Chicago University Press.

ARIES, P. (1962) *Centuries of Childhood*. London: Cape. (translated from the French by R. Baldick).

ARMYTAGE, W.H.G. (1961) *Heavens Below: Utopian experiments in England 1560–1960*. London: Routledge and Kegan Paul.

AXTELL, J.L. (1968) *The Educational Writings of John Locke*. London: Cambridge University Press.

BAMFORD, T.W. (1970) *Thomas Arnold on Education*. Cambridge: Cambridge University Press.

BORER, M.C. (1976) *Willingly to School: a history of women's education*. Guildford: Lutterworth.

BRAUER, G.C. (1959) *The Education of a Gentleman: theories of gentlemanly education in England. 1660–1775*. New York: Bookman Associates.

BURSTYN, J.N. (1980) *Victorian Education and the Ideal of Womanhood.* London: Croom Helm: Totowa, N.J.: Barnes and Noble.

CARDWELL, D.S.L. (1957) *The Organisation of Science in England: a retrospect.* London: Heinemann.

CHAYTOR, H.J. (1945) *From Script to Print. An introduction to medieval literature.* Cambridge: Cambridge University Press.

CIPOLLA, C.P. (1969) *Literacy and Development in the West.* Harmondsworth: Penguin.

CLANCHY, M.T. (1979) *From Memory to Written Record: England 1066–1307.* London: Edward Arnold.

CLARKE, M.L. (1959) *Classical Education in Britain, 1500–1900.* Cambridge: Cambridge University Press.

COLLINS, P. (1963) *Dickens and Education.* London: Macmillan.

CONNELL, W.F. (1950) *The Educational Thought and Influence of Matthew Arnold.* London: Routledge and Kegan Paul.

COTGROVE, S.F. (1958) *Technical Education and Social Change.* London: Allen and Unwin.

COVENEY, P. (1967) *The Image of Childhood.* Harmondsworth: Penguin.

DEANESLY, M. (1969) *A History of the Medieval Church, 590–1500.* London: Methuen.

DOBINSON, C.H. (1969) *Jean Jacques Rousseau: his thought and its relevance today.* London: Methuen.

DUCKETT, E.S. (1957) *Alfred the Great and his England.* London: Collins.

FLEXNER, E. (1972) *Mary Wollstonecraft.* New York: Coward, McCann and Geoghegan.

GARDINER, D. (1929) *English Girlhood at School: a study of women's education through twelve centuries.* Cambridge: Cambridge University Press.

GORDON, P. and WHITE, J. (1979) *Philosophers as Educational Reformers: the influence of idealism on British educational thought and practice.* London: Routledge and Kegan Paul.

ILLICH, I.D. (1971) *Deschooling Society.* London: Calder.

KAMM, J. (1965) *Hope Deferred: girls' education in English history.* London: Methuen.

KELLY, T. (1957) *George Birkbeck: pioneer of adult education.* Liverpool: Liverpool University Press.

MAUSE, L. de (ed.) (1976) *The History of Childhood.* London: Souvenir (E and A) Press.

PETERS, R.S. (1966) *Ethics and Education.* London: Allen and Unwin.

PINCHBECK, I. and HEWITT, M. (1969, 1973) *Children in English Society, 2 vols.* London: Routledge and Kegan Paul.

REIMER, E. (1971) *School is Dead: an essay on alternatives in education.* Harmondsworth: Penguin.

RODERICK, G.W. (1967) *The Emergence of a Scientific Society.* London: Macmillan.

RUSK, R.R. (1969) *The Doctrines of the Great Educators.* London: Macmillan.

RYDER, J. and SILVER, H. (1977) *Modern English Society.* London: Methuen.

SADLER, J.E. (1966) *J.A. Comenius and the Concept of Universal Education.* London: Allen and Unwin.

SILVER, H. (ed.) (1969) *Robert Owen on Education.* London: Cambridge University Press.

SILVER, H. (ed.) (1973) *Equal Opportunity in Education: a reader in social class and educational opportunity.* London: Methuen.

SILVER, H. (1980) *Education and the Social Condition.* London: Methuen.

SOUTHERN, R.W. (1970) *Western Society and the Church in the Middle Ages.* Harmondsworth: Penguin.

STEWART, W.A.C. (1972) *Progressives and Radicals in English Education, 1750–1970.* London: Macmillan.

WIENER, M.J. (1981) *English Culture and the decline of the Industrial Spirit, 1850–1980.* Cambridge: Cambridge University Press.

WILLIAMS, G. (1979) *Religion, Language and Nationality in Wales.* Cardiff: University of Wales Press.

WILLIAMS, R. (1958) *Culture and Society, 1780–1950.* London: Chatto and Windus.

WILLIAMS, R. (1961) *The Long Revolution.* London: Chatto and Windus.

Chapter 3

ALDRICH, R. (1979) *Sir John Pakington and National Education.* Leeds: University of Leeds.

BARKER, R. (1972) *Education and Politics 1900–1951: a study of the Labour Party.* Oxford: Clarendon Press.

BEALES, A.C.F. (1963) *Education under Penalty: English Catholic education from the Reformation to the fall of James II, 1547–1689.* London: Athlone Press.

BINNS, H.B. (1908) *A Century of Education: being the centenary history of the British and Foreign School Society, 1808–1908.* London: Dent.

BISHOP, A.S. (1971) *The Rise of a Central Authority for English Education.* Cambridge: Cambridge University Press.

BURGESS, H.J. (1958) *Enterprise in Education: the story of the work of the Established Church in the education of the people prior to 1870.* London: National Society; SPCK.

CASTLE, E.B. (1970) *The Teacher.* London: Oxford University Press.

CLARKE, W.K.L. (1959) *A History of the SPCK.* London: SPCK.

CRUICKSHANK, M. (1963) *Church and State in English Education: 1870 to the present day.* London: Macmillan.

DENT, H.C. (1977) *The Training of Teachers in England and Wales. 1800–1975.* London: Hodder and Stoughton.

EAGLESHAM, E.J.R. (1956) *From School Board to Local Authority.* London: Routledge and Kegan Paul.

EAGLESHAM, E.J.R. (1967) *The Foundations of Twentieth-Century Education in England.* London: Routledge and Kegan Paul.

FENWICK, K. and McBRIDE, P. (1981) *The Government of Education.* Oxford: Robertson.

FLETCHER, S. (1980) *Feminists and Bureaucrats: a study in the development of girls' education in the nineteenth century.* Cambridge: Cambridge University Press.

GORDON, P. (1974) *The Victorian School Manager: a study in the management of education 1800–1902.* London: Woburn.

GORDON, P. and LAWTON, D. (1978) *Curriculum Change in the Nineteenth and*

Twentieth Centuries. London: Hodder and Stoughton.

GOSDEN, P.H.J.H. (1966)*The Development of Educational Administration in England and Wales*. Oxford: Blackwell.

GOSDEN. P.H.J.H. (1972) *The Evolution of a Profession*: *a study of the contribution of teachers' associations to the development of school teaching as a professional occupation*. Oxford: Blackwell.

GOSDEN, P.H.J.H. (1976) *Education in the Second World War*: *a study in policy and administration*. London: Methuen.

GOSDEN, P.H.J.H. and SHARP, P.R. (1978) *The Development of an Education Service*: *the West Riding 1889–1974*. Oxford: Robertson.

GRACE, G. (1978) *Teachers, Ideology and Control*: *a study in urban education*. London: Routledge and Kegan Paul.

GREEN, V.H.H. (1964) *Religion at Oxford and Cambridge*. London: SCM.

HISTORY OF EDUCATION SOCIETY (1970) *Studies in the Government and Control of Education since 1860*. London: Methuen.

HISTORY OF EDUCATION SOCIETY (1973) *Education and the Professions*. London: Methuen.

HURT, J. (1971) *Education in Evolution*: *Church, State, Society and Popular Education 1800–1870*. London: Hart-Davies.

LAWRENCE, B. (1972) *The Administration of Education in Britain*. London: Batsford.

LEESE, J. (1950) *Personalities and Power in English Education*. Leeds: E.J. Arnold.

MONTGOMERY, R.J. (1965) *Examinations*: *An Account of their Evolution as Administrative Devices in England*. London: Longman.

MURPHY, J. (1971) *Church, State and Schools in Britain, 1800–1970*. London: Routledge and Kegan Paul.

PAZ, D.G. (1980) *The Politics of Working-Class Education in Britain, 1830–50*. Manchester: Manchester University Press.

PERKIN, H.J. (1969) *Key Profession*: *the history of the Association of University Teachers*. London: Routledge and Kegan Paul.

ROACH, J. (1971) *Public Examinations in England, 1850–1900*. Cambridge: Cambridge University Press.

SEABORNE, M. (1971, 1977) *The English School*: *its architecture and organisation*. London: Routledge and Kegan Paul. (2 vols, second vol. with R.Lowe)

SMITH, F. (1923) *The Life and Work of Sir James Kay-Shuttleworth*. London: John Murray.

SUTHERLAND, G. (ed.) (1972) *Studies in the Growth of Nineteenth-Century Government*. London: Routledge and Kegan Paul.

SUTHERLAND, G. (1973) *Policy-Making in Elementary Education 1870–1895*. London: Oxford University Press.

SYLVESTER, D.W. (1974) *Robert Lowe and Education*. London: Cambridge University Press.

TROPP, A. (1957) *The School Teachers*: *the growth of the teaching profession in England and Wales from 1800 to the present day*. London: Heinemann.

VINCENT, W.A.L. (1950) *The State and School Education 1640–1660 in England and Wales*. London: SPCK.

WEST, E.G. (1970) *Education and the State*: *a study in political economy*. London: Institute of Economic Affairs.

YOUNG, M.F.D. (ed.) (1971) *Knowledge and Control: new directions for the sociology of education*. London: Collier-Macmillan.

Chapter 4

ADAMS, F. (1882) *History of the Elementary School Contest in England*. London: Chapman and Hall (1970 reprint, Bath: Chivers for Library Association).

BENNETT, N. *et al*. (1976) *Teaching Styles and Pupil Progress*. London: Open Books.

GOLDSTROM, J.M. (1972) *The Social Content of Education, 1808–1870: a study of the working-class school reader in England and Ireland*. Shannon: Irish University Press.

HURT, J.S. (1979) *Elementary Schooling and the Working Classes, 1860–1918*. London: Routledge and Kegan Paul.

ISAACS, S. (1930) *Intellectual Growth in Young Children*. London: Routledge and Kegan Paul.

ISAACS, S. (1933) *Social Development in Young Children*. London: Routledge and Kegan Paul.

JONES, M.G. (1938) *The Charity School Movement: a study of eighteenth-century Puritanism in action*. London: Cambridge University Press (1964 reprint, London: Cass).

LAQUEUR, T.W. (1976) *Religion and Respectability: Sunday schools and working class culture 1780–1850*. New Haven, London: Yale University Press.

McCANN, P. (ed.) (1977) *Popular Education and Socialization in the Nineteenth Century*. London: Methuen.

McLEISH, J. (1969) *Evangelical Religion and Popular Education: a modern interpretation*. London: Methuen.

NEUBERG, V.E. (1971) *Popular Education in Eighteenth-Century England*. London: Woburn.

ORME, N. (1973) *English Schools in the Middle Ages*. London: Methuen.

PETERS, R.S. (ed.) (1969) *Perspectives on Plowden*. London: Routledge and Kegan Paul.

ROBSON, A.H. (1931) *The Education of Children engaged in Industry in England 1833–1876*. London: Routledge and Kegan Paul, Trench, Trubner.

SELLECK, R.J.W. (1968) *The New Education: the English background 1870–1914*. Melbourne, London: Pitman.

SELLECK, R.J.W. (1972) *English Primary Education and the Progressives, 1914–1939*. London: Routledge and Kegan Paul.

SILVER, H. (1965) *The Concept of Popular Education: a study of ideas and social movements in the early nineteenth century*. London: MacGibbon and Kee.

SILVER, P. and SILVER, H. (1974) *The Education of the Poor: the history of a National school 1824–1974*. London: Routledge and Kegan Paul.

SMITH, F. (1931) *A History of English Elementary Education 1760–1902*. London: University of London Press.

STURT, M. (1967) *The Education of the People: a history of primary education in England and Wales in the nineteenth century.* London: Routledge and Kegan Paul.

SUTHERLAND, G. (1971) *Elementary Education in the Nineteenth Century.* London: Historical Association.

THOMPSON, A.H. (1942) *Song-Schools in the Middle Ages.* London: Church Music Society.

WARDLE, D. (1976) *English Popular Education 1780–1975.* Cambridge: Cambridge University Press.

WHITBREAD, N. (1972) *The Evolution of the Nursery-Infant School: a history of infant and nursery education in Britain, 1800–1970.* London: Routledge and Kegan Paul.

Chapter 5

ARCHER, R.L. (1921) *Secondary Education in the Nineteenth Century.* Cambridge: Cambridge University Press. (1966 reprint, London: Cass).

BAMFORD, T.W. (1960) *Thomas Arnold.* London: Cresset.

BAMFORD, T.W. (1967) *The Rise of the Public Schools.* London: Nelson.

BANKS, O. (1955) *Parity and Prestige in English Secondary Education.* London: Routledge and Kegan Paul.

BRYANT, M. (1979) *The Unexpected Revolution. A Study in the History of the Education of Women and Girls in the Nineteenth Century.* London: University of London Institute of Education.

FENWICK I.G.K. (1976) *The Comprehensive School 1944–1970.* London: Methuen.

GATHORNE-HARDY, J. (1977) *The Public School Phenomenon 597–1977.* London: Hodder and Stoughton.

GRAVES, J.T.R. (1943) *Policy and Progress in Secondary Education 1902–1942.* London: Nelson.

GORDON, P. (1980) *Selection for Secondary Education.* London: Woburn.

HEENEY, B. (1969) *Mission to the Middle Classes: the Woodard Schools 1848–1891.* London: SPCK.

HONEY, J.R. de S. (1977) *Tom Brown's Universe: The Development of the Public School in the 19th Century.* London: Millington.

KAMM, J. (1958) *How Different from Us. A Biography of Miss Buss and Miss Beale.* London: The Bodley Head.

KAMM, J. (1971) *Indicative Past. A Hundred Years of the Girls' Public Day School Trust.* London: Allen and Unwin.

KAYE, E, (1972) *A History of Queen's College, London 1848–1972.* London: Chatto and Windus.

LAWSON, J. (1963) *A Town Grammar School through Six Centuries: a history of Hull grammar school against its local background.* London: Oxford University Press.

LEACH, A.F. (1896) *English Schools at the Reformation 1546–8.* London: Constable. (1968 reprint, New York: Russell).

LEACH, A.F. (1915) *The Schools of Medieval England.* London: Methuen.

LINDSAY, K. (1926) *Social Progress and Educational Waste.* London: Routledge and Kegan Paul.

MACK, E.C. (1938) *Public Schools and British Opinion, 1780–1860*. London: Methuen.

MACK, E.C. (1941) *Public Schools and British Opinion since 1860*. New York: Columbia University Press.

MUMFORD, A.A. (1919) *The Manchester Grammar School 1515–1915: a regional study of the advancement of learning in Manchester since the Reformation*. London: Longmans, Green.

ORME, N. (1973) *English Schools in the Middle Ages*. London: Methuen.

PERCIVAL, A.C. (1973) *Very Superior Men: Some early Public School Headmasters and their Achievements*. London: Knight.

RUBINSTEIN, D. and SIMON, B. (1969) *The Evolution of the Comprehensive School 1926–1966*. London: Routledge and Kegan Paul.

SIMON, B. and BRADLEY, I. (eds.) (1975) *The Victorian Public School*. Dublin: Gill and MacMillan,

SKIDELSKY, R. (1969) *English Progressive Schools*. Harmondsworth: Penguin.

TAWNEY, R.H. (1922) *Secondary Education for All*. London: Labour Party; Allen and Unwin.

TAYLOR, W. (1963) *The Secondary Modern School*. London: Faber and Faber.

TOMPSON, R.S. (1971) *Classics or Charity? The dilemma of the 18th century grammar school*. Manchester: Manchester University Press.

VINCENT, W.A.L. (1969) *The Grammar Schools. Their Continuing Tradition 1660–1714*. London: Murray.

WALLIS, P.J. (1966) *Histories of Old Schools: a revised list for England and Wales*. Newcastle upon Tyne: University.

WATSON, F. (1908) *The English Grammar Schools to 1660: their curriculum and practice*. Cambridge: Cambridge University Press.

WATSON, F. (1909) *The Beginnings of the teaching of Modern Subjects in England*. London: Pitman. (1971 reprint, Wakefield: S.R. Publishers).

Chapter 6

ARGLES, M. (1964) *South Kensington to Robbins: an account of English technical and scientific education since 1851*. London: Longman.

ARMYTAGE, W.H.G. (1955) *Civic Universities,* London: Benn.

BELLOT, H.H. (1929) *University College, London, 1826–1926*. London: University Press.

BRADBROOK, M.C. (1969) *'That Infidel Place', A Short History of Girton College 1869–1969*. London: Chatto and Windus.

CHARLTON, H.B. (1952) *Portrait of a University 1851–1951, to commemorate the Centenary of Manchester University*. Manchester: Manchester University Press.

COBBAN, A.B. (1969) *The King's Hall within the University of Cambridge in the later Middle Ages*. London: Cambridge University Press.

COBBAN, A.B. (1975) *The Medieval Universities: their development and organisation*. London: Methuen.

CURTIS, M.H. (1959) *Oxford and Cambridge in Transition, 1558–1642: an essay on changing relations between the English universities and English society*. Oxford: Clarendon Press.

DENT, H.C. (1961) *Universities in Transition.* London: Cohen and West.

DONALDSON, L. (1975) *Policy and the Polytechnics: pluralistic drift in higher education.* Farnborough: Saxon House.

ELLIS, E.L. (1972) *The University College of Wales, Aberystwyth 1872–1972.* Cardiff: University of Wales Press.

ELLIS, T.I. (1935) *The Development of Higher Education in Wales.* Wrexham: Hughes.

GREEN, V.H.H. (1969) *The Universities.* Harmondsworth: Penguin.

GREEN, V.H.H. (1974) *A History of Oxford University.* London: Batsford.

HACKETT, M.B. (1970) *The Original Statutes of Cambridge University.* London: Cambridge University Press.

HARRISON, J.F.C. (1961) *Learning and Living, 1790–1960: a study in the history of the English adult education movement.* London: Routledge and Kegan Paul.

HEARNSHAW, J.F.C. (1929) *The Centenary History of King's College, London, 1828–1928.* London: Harrap.

HUELIN, G. (1978) *King's College, London 1828–1978.* London: King's College.

KEARNEY, H. (1970) *Scholars and Gentlemen: universities and society in pre-industrial Britain 1500–1700.* London: Faber.

KELLY, T. (1962) *A History of Adult Education in Great Britain.* Liverpool: Liverpool University Press.

KNOWLES, D. (1948, 1955, 1959) *The Religious Orders in England* (3 vols). Cambridge: Cambridge University Press.

LYONS, H. (1944) *The Royal Society 1660–1940: a history of its administration under its charters.* London: Cambridge University Press (1968 reprint, New York: Greenwood).

McLACHLAN, H. (1931) *English Education under the Test Acts, being the History of the Nonconformist Academies 1662–1820.* Manchester: Manchester University Press.

McLACHLAN, H. (1943) *Warrington Academy: its history and influence.* Manchester: Chetham Society.

MALLETT, C.E. (1924–7) *A History of the University of Oxford* (3 vols). London: Methuen. (1968 reprint London: Methuen).

MOUNTFORD, J. (1966) *British Universities.* London: Oxford University Press.

PARKER, I. (1914) *Dissenting Academies in England.* Cambridge: Cambridge University Press. (1969 reprint New York: Octagon).

PERRY, W. (1976) *Open University.* Milton Keynes: Open University Press.

POWER, E. (1922) *Medieval English Nunneries c. 1275 to 1535.* Cambridge: Cambridge University Press. (1964 reprint New York: Biblo and (Tannen).

PREST, W.R. (1972) *The Inns of Court under Elizabeth I and the early Stuarts 1590–1640.* London: Longman.

PRICE, D.T.W. (1977) *A History of St. David's University College, Lampeter.* Cardiff: University of Wales Press.

RASHDALL, H. (1936) *The Universities of Europe in the Middle Ages.* London: Oxford University Press (3 vols. edited by F.M. Powicke and A.B. Emden).

ROBINSON, E.E. (1968) *The New Polytechnics.* Harmondsworth: Penguin.

RODERICK, G.W. and STEPHENS, M.D. (1972) *Scientific and Technical Education in Nineteenth-Century England.* Newton Abbot: David and Charles.

ROTHBLATT, S. (1968) *The Revolution of the Dons: Cambridge and Society in Victorian England.* London: Faber.

SANDERSON, M. (1972) *The Universities and British Industry 1850–1970.* London: Routledge and Kegan Paul.

SANDERSON, M. (ed.) (1975) *The Universities in the Nineteenth Century.* London: Routledge and Kegan Paul.

SMITH, J.W.A. (1954)) *The Birth of Modern Education: the contribution of the Dissenting Academies 1660–1800.* London: Independent Press.

TREASE, G. (1967) *The Grand Tour.* London: Heinemann.

TUKE, M.J. (1939) *A History of Bedford College for Women 1849–1937.* Oxford: Oxford University Press.

TYLECOTE, M. (1957) *The Mechanics' Institutes of Lancashire and Yorkshire before 1851.* Manchester: Manchester University Press.

WEBSTER, C. (1976) *The Great Instauration: Science, Medicine and Reform 1626–1660.* New York: Holmes and Meier.

WHITING, C.E. (1932) *The University of Durham, 1832–1932.* London: Sheldon.

WINSTANLEY, D.A. (1922) *The University of Cambridge in the Eighteenth Century.* Cambridge University Press.

WINSTANLEY, D.A. (1935) *Unreformed Cambridge.* Cambridge: Cambridge University Press. (1977 reprint, New York: Arno).

WINSTANLEY, D.A. (1940) *Early Victorian Cambridge.* Cambridge: Cambridge University Press.

WINSTANLEY, D.A. (1947) *Later Victorian Cambridge.* Cambridge: Cambridge University Press.

INDEX